Praise for
A Life Made from Scratch

"As a former colleague in Congress, I was always impressed with Marie's remarkable journey through her family, business, and political challenges. Her story is inspirational but also instructive to those looking to make a pivot in their lives. Her stories are interesting, refreshingly honest, and helpful."

—Congressman Ro Khanna, CA-17

"How often do you get to read a book that entertains, enlightens, and energizes in equal doses? Marie Newman's *A Life Made from Scratch* grabs you from the jump and just keeps grabbing until you're genuinely bummed it's over. Dealing with bullies from her children's playground to the nation's capital, Marie has been through it. But there's zero woe-is-me stuff in here. With a warm, witty, and welcoming tone, Marie deftly weaves personal and professional stories that are soul-bearing—at times heart-crushing—and ultimately inspiring and uplifting. But wait, there's more! It's chock-full of practical advice and action-oriented game plans for people of all personalities, ages, and professions. Marie is a next-level champion of underdogs (and actual dogs), and her motivating memoir is a must-have manual for anyone who wants to make their world better—internally, locally, and globally."

—Lisa K. Nelson, television writer and producer for Amazon, Netflix, Sony, and others

"If you have this book, it will be like a best friend. You'll never feel alone. Marie gives you the courage to do something you've always wanted to try even if it's daunting and provides the specifics of how to get it done. This book talks to you in a way that you'll find immersive, surprising, and deeply personal."

—Jodee Blanco, *New York Times* bestselling author of *Please Stop Laughing at Me* and speaker

"The story of Marie's improbable journey from reluctant activist to politician-on-a-mission is filled with robust lessons and an inside look into being a change agent while in Congress. Her personal stories are inspirational, and the political revelations are instructive and eye-opening. A fascinating read."

—Ryan Grim, author, journalist, and bureau chief at The Intercept

"In *A Life Made from Scratch*, readers will find wisdom, humor, transparency, a dash of therapy, and a dose of Chicago politics. As Marie tells her story, she reveals herself as both tough and tender, recounting her time as a CEO, US congresswoman, and fierce Mama Bear. This inspiring memoir will leave you feeling positive and motivated. Each chapter is summed up with a lesson, concrete steps to achieve it, and overall takeaways to help readers put their dreams into action. A must-read for anyone who wants to pivot their life."

—Lisa Katzenberger, award-winning author

"Newman's memoir is truly from the heart. She takes us from the halls of Congress, where she flees insurrectionists, to her living room, where she has emotional conversations with her struggling trans child, to her car, where she cries about the state of the world only to pick herself back up and continue fighting for change. This is the book you need to remember that you can get through hard times and always come out the other side stronger."

—Jack L. Turban, MD, MHS, director of the UCSF Gender Psychiatry Program and author of *Free to Be: Understanding Kids & Gender Identity*

"Marie Newman has lived an eclectic and wide-ranging life: wife, mother, entrepreneur, politician. In her new book, *A Life Made from Scratch*, Newman explores the rewards and cost of living a big life, especially if one is focused on empathy, fairness, and service. A Life Made from Scratch is part memoir, part self-help book, and in it, Newman is, at turns, raw and vulnerable, humorous and self-deprecating. In her fiercest mom mode, she lays out a blueprint that all of us might follow, which gives permission to try and fail and try again. But always with a thought of doing better, being better."

—Rita Woods, author

"Marie Newman, in her memoir, *A Life Made from Scratch*, weaves her most authentic personal stories regarding family, change, diversity, challenges, transitions, and profound love in advocating for her children. She addresses all adversity directly, with an inspiring intentionality that is reflected in her work and very successful political career. In this way, parenting and politics pivot and rise purposefully in a distinct metaphor for resilience matched by a work ethic that knows no limits. The 'coach' in Marie utilizes teaching methods at the end of each chapter that draw the reader in further. We all live lives 'from scratch.' It's the beauty of uncertainty Newman embraces again and again with a sense of humility that makes this memoir so brilliant. Does anyone have wine?"

—"Coach P," Joanne P. McCallie, head coach at Duke University

"*A Life Made from Scratch* is a powerful and emotional read as Marie Newman takes you on some of the most important journeys of her life. She shares her encounters with bullies (both for her son and herself) and also the experience of raising a transgender daughter. *A Life Made from Scratch* shows that you can 'build your future from scratch' every day and provides not only her own relatable life examples but also lessons, hows, and takeaways at the end of every chapter. I really enjoyed Marie's story and her look into how to pivot in life, her journey in politics, and building a life from scratch."

—Holly J Mayes, author of *Dream, Girl: A Memoir*

"If you want to learn how to be an advocate, a true champion, you must read Marie Newman's *A Life Made from Scratch*. This memoir portrays the challenges confronted by someone who is a powerful voice for those often victimized by others, for many years speaking out against bullying and antitrans, antigay voices. Her advocacy may have begun close to home, with her love and commitment to her children, but that advocacy expanded. Her career as a congresswoman from Illinois was only a single term, but she made a difference in the lives of others well beyond her district. She bravely spoke up in times and about controversial topics when others were cowed by more well-funded forces. Congresswoman Newman has had many careers—as an advertising executive, a nonprofit CEO, and a politician. A Life Made from Scratch will both inspire and challenge you to take your own actions to make the world a better place."

—Barbara Gitenstein, university president

"*A Life Made from Scratch* is one of those books that sticks with you. I felt a sense of camaraderie with the author's experiences and how she makes big solutions 'from scratch.' I feel like her challenges and how she managed through them were very relatable, inspirational, and uplifting, providing a real sense of how-to. Her stories are charming and informative."

—Douglas Keane, chef

"In *A Life Made from Scratch*, Marie Newman brings the same wisdom, wit, and fierce commitment to justice to the page that she does to halls of power. A joyous and enlightening read."

—Brian C. Johnson, CEO of Equality Illinois

"Marie Newman's *A Life Made from Scratch* is an inspiring and authentic account of a leader who has dedicated her life to championing social justice, equity, and the everyday needs of all people. With raw and unfiltered honesty, Newman takes readers behind the scenes of her tireless work in building coalitions, forging unlikely partnerships, and overcoming immense obstacles to create meaningful change—all without compromising her values and principles. Her passion for uplifting communities shines through every page, making the book both refreshing and deeply moving. It's a must-read for anyone who believes in the power of grassroots action and the importance of standing up for what's right, no matter the odds. It's also a must-read for those who are feeling hopeless in these trying times because it offers a path to meaningful progress. Newman's story is a testament to the idea that, with determination and compassion, we can truly move mountains."

—Qasim Rashid, international humanitarian and human rights attorney

"Marie Newman's memoir, *A Life Made from Scratch*, is a powerful testament to political transformation and personal courage. As a fellow advocate for gun safety, I'm thrilled to endorse this honest account of Marie's journey from activist to congresswoman. Marie's story of resilience—from challenging the political establishment to defeating a long-entrenched incumbent to fighting for meaningful reforms—is a must-read for anyone who wants to understand how authentic advocacy can reshape our political landscape."

—Shannon Watts, author, organizer, and founder of Moms Demand Action

A Life Made from Scratch
by Marie Newman

© Copyright 2025 Marie Newman

ISBN 979-8-88824-658-0

All rights reserved. No part of this publication may be reproduced, stored in a retrieval system, or transmitted in any form or by any means—electronic, mechanical, photocopy, recording, or any other—except for brief quotations in printed reviews, without the prior written permission of the author.

Edited by Miranda Dillon
Cover design by Catherine Herold

Published by

3705 Shore Drive
Virginia Beach, VA 23455
800-435-4811
www.koehlerbooks.com

A Life Made from Scratch

LESSONS FROM A CONTROVERSIAL COGRESSWOMAN, MOMPRENEUR AND UNSTOPPABLE ACTIVIST

Marie Newman

VIRGINIA BEACH
CAPE CHARLES

Dedication

To my incredibly brilliant, patient, and loving husband. Without his unwavering loyalty, kindness, and belief in me, this story and life would have never happened. He has empowered me to tackle my every dream in the last thirty years, so that I would never have a regret in life. And this is why I love him more than anyone can imagine.

My deepest thanks and love go to Margie, my best friend, a great human being, a sage of life, for always making me laugh.

Forever love to my two sisters, who are loving, kind, always supportive, no matter what, and always there when needed, no matter what.

To Jodee and Ann, my writing coaches and sounding boards, you are simply the best. I appreciate them more than they can ever know.

Finally, this book is for all women struggling to find a solution, purpose, or how to pivot. I'm rooting for you!

Introduction

"You become. It takes a long time. That's why it doesn't happen often to people who break easily, or have sharp edges, or who have to be carefully kept. Generally, by the time you are Real, most of your hair has been loved off, and your eyes drop out and you get loose in your joints and very shabby."

—Margery Williams, *The Velveteen Rabbit*

I SHARE THIS PASSAGE because we all "become" something; we are constantly evolving and changing. Part of that process is to know when it is time to make a change, pivot, solve a challenge, or build something from scratch. Part of becoming you is accepting that *you* must solve a problem or discern when to build something from scratch. People need lots of help along the way, but the decision to initiate a change is typically up to *you* and not *we*.

I wrote this book to help those who are at a crossroads in life. You may be interested in a life pivot or have realized that you need to build a life solution from scratch to solve a problem because the solution does not currently exist. Accepting this as a natural part of life and believing that God, the universe, or Mother Nature wants you to do something is part of your growth. Humans don't just evolve magically; we evolve based on a desire or need to evolve. We adapt.

Change is hard for everyone, even a card-carrying "change-aholic" like me. That said, we must change, pivot, and build to have a higher quality of life and grow and advance as a society. Do not fear the pivot or the daunting task of building something from scratch. Embrace it! Love it! Even if you love it so much, its floppy ears are loved right off!

Preface

MY GOAL IN writing this book is to help readers understand a few things. 1. Building your own solutions from scratch to solve the thorniest problems in your life is rewarding and effective. 2. Politicians of all stripes are just human beings, warts and all. 3. There is no denying that women, people of color, LGBTQ+ folks, and folks with disabilities are faced with greater pushback, more discrimination, and being overlooked more than White men. We need to not just *understand* but *change that dynamic*. 4. Learn to speak up and out, especially to power. 5. Advocate for yourself. Do not tolerate gaslighting or bullying.

What is *not* my goal is to hurt folks here. A few people from my personal life have been renamed in the following pages so that they are not called out in any way. Similarly, while my goal is to share how, why, and what we can do to help people build from scratch, the mandate here is not to shame, humiliate, or be unkind, but it is important to know specific things I've encountered along my journey. Many others have encountered the same. The consequences of our society, communities, and political structures acting as bullies are long-lasting and hurtful. The truth does not need to hurt; it can be instructive.

Hopefully, we are all learning together and can see where we have challenges and how to improve. The following chapters are a series of life events that helped me evolve to where I am and who I am supposed to be.

Candor and kindness can live together. We can tell the truth and learn from it.

PART ONE:

Lessons from Bullies and Mentors

CHAPTER ONE

Hold My Damn Wine

"**Mom, I think** I know how to stop the bullying at school. I can get into a horrible car accident, and then I can come back as a different person," my angel-eyed oldest child blurted out one day out of nowhere. Can you imagine hearing that from your super bright, innocent eleven-year-old? It has to get really bad at school for someone so young to say something so troubling, don't you think? Well, it was my own son, Quinn, who said it. Hearing those words come out of my baby's mouth absolutely leveled me. I could feel my whole heart break. I knew I had to act. This was the turning point. My perfect family, my perfect little town, my beautiful home, and my perfect life really was not (and never was), well, perfect. In fact, there were many events over the years that had messed with the fairy tale I had made up in my mind. But on the day Quinn dropped that bombshell, I not only accepted that the fairy tale was not true, but I also knew I could make it better. I was certain.

Up until that point, our family was living the dream in my Mayberry-like little suburb. (Not really, but I liked to think it was an ordinary, pastoral, middle-class existence). From the time my kids were born up until the time my oldest started to suffer from bullying, I really thought our problems were ordinary and what we now call "first-world problems." And they were, but things would get a little tougher.

This time in my life would be one of many when solutions took a great deal of time and were not readily available to me. I frequently felt completely out of control over my family's destiny, and I knew there was no manual or guidebook. It was quite clear I would have to build something from scratch.

Our lovely little suburb was filled with gorgeous trees, parks, and a tranquil, beloved lake at its heart. (We moved away thirteen years ago now, but when I think of it, I still remember how green and filled with sunshine it was.) Granted, some folks living there were more competitive and social-climby than I liked, but we had many lovely, salt-of-the-earth and kind friends too. We were happy and had all the little problems most families generally have. My husband worked very hard with long hours and had a narcissistic, childish boss. My small consulting business had its ebbs and flows. We had day-care challenges, and we were always trying to make sure the kids were happy and healthy. My oldest was very smart, with near-perfect grades, but overly sensitive at times, anxious, and quirky, which meant he had some social problems. My youngest was mischievous at school, and I frequently had to go into school to deal with it. All sorts of ordinary stuff, I thought.

I can remember the first time I witnessed Quinn being bullied. I just never knew how bad it would get after that. I saw a group of kids in his second-grade class, whom both Quinn and I knew, running into a huddle in the park, scooping up sand from the sandbox with raccoon poop in it, and throwing it at Quinn while calling him a "retarded loser."

On a regular basis, Quinn told me about humiliating things kids did to him throughout third and fourth grades. I'm not talking about pranks or light humor. Telling him straight up that he was weird, irritating, or hated, weekly. Often, he was ignored and left out of social things. When out playing with kids, sometimes they told him to meet them somewhere, and when Quinn showed up, he was alone. Quinn came home, telling me, "It happened again." It often bothered me more than it seemed to bother him. It made me cry. Thank God he had a few truly wonderful friends who were kind and lovely. He is still close to them today, and I love them like sons.

A popular bullying tool is to start rumors. One of the lieutenant bullies took it upon himself to make up three sets of rumors about my son. One involved wetting his pants, another asserted that he was mentally challenged/autistic, and another was that he had never had a friend. This bully then proceeded to seed these rumors across the third and fourth grade classes. It was clear this was effective because parents in town started to express their sadness about Quinn's "issue" to me on the regular.

Here's some backstory. When Quinn was four to seven years old, he had many sensory issues, some social issues, and anxiety. We had him tested several times, and he never registered on the autism spectrum, but he definitely had some features that could appear to be Asperger's syndrome, but it was not a diagnosis at all. Honestly, in some ways, life may have been much easier if Quinn had actually been on the spectrum because we would have known a little better how to manage it. I think it would have been a clearer and more direct path. We would ultimately find or build all the solutions needed, but it took several years.

The day I will remember intensely forever still sets my hair on fire. At a football practice in fifth grade, the head bully at the time, who was a very good athlete but truly an absolute asshole of a kid (there, I said it—I'm sorry if that offends, but it was true), encouraged a group of boys to talk like developmentally challenged kids and harass my son for three hours straight during practice. They called him "retarded," "freak," and "geek" and sang a song they made up to torture him. Quinn came home that night, took a shovel from the garage, and just went to town hitting our garage with it while swearing up a storm. My husband stood up from the couch to stop him, and I said, "No, let him let it out." He did, and the three of us stayed up all night and cried together. Early on in our kids' lives, I told them they could swear when really upset, but not all the time. I do not regret that at all. *Psst. Swearing helps me when I'm upset too.*

I remember inviting the head bully's parents over to calmly discuss how we might solve this issue. It was excruciating, Mayberry-style. We invited them in and initiated small talk. Then, we laid out the ways and specific instances in which their son bullied our son. Bully's father, a former big-jock dude living vicariously through his eleven-year-old son, said, "I think this is a misunderstanding. Kids will be kids. Boys will be boys."

I shared, "That may be, but your son has been strategically and methodically humiliating my son for over a year."

Bully Mom, with perfect hair and perfect jeans, responded, "Oh gosh, our son is so sweet. I just don't see it, Marie."

"Well, let me assist you with seeing it," I responded with a condescending smile.

I pulled out a notebook filled with documented incidents—dates, times, and specifics. Mom Bully shifted in her seat uncomfortably as I recited the instances. Bully Dad's eyes glazed over, and he began to tense his jaw and shoulders. My husband chimed in with colorful commentary, very calmly but firmly. The best both bully parents could manage to say was this: "Well, we are terribly sorry to hear your son is offended by our son's sense of humor. Nobody else is at school. But we will talk to him."

As our parting words at the door, we said, "We appreciate your help, but let me be super crystal clear. I am watching and recording." They left, Mrs. Bully clutching her chunky cool-mom necklace. I closed the door and said to my husband, "Oh my God, Stepford wives much! What a pretentious bitch. Yuck!" To be clear, I am not always Betsy Bubbles; my tongue is blade sharp, and I am not afraid to use it.

While things seemed to get better for a while, the issue did not go away.

Sometimes in life, the fire finds me, but sometimes I find the fire. This time, it was both.

My baby was hurting, and I was not f-ing having it anymore!

During all of this, teachers continued to report that Quinn was incredibly bright, received excellent grades, and was a gifted musician, but he had trouble "fitting in" with other kids. We pushed through fifth grade with great tenacity. Quinn had a couple of real friends, but we found that they were bullied often because they were friends with Quinn. We tried to find new friends for Quinn outside of school. We enrolled him in clubs, activities, camps, and programs with some success. Literally, we tried everything to reduce or stop the bullying. Nothing was helping.

Then came the day I will never forget. Quinn came home with that idea about "getting into a horrible accident and becoming a new person." I knew there was no going back for me. I took my mama-badass sword-and-shield set out of the closet and never looked back. In these situations, when I have decided to address a fire, my husband gets anxious because he is conflict avoidant, and I am conflict "addressant." I confided in a close friend whose son was in a different grade and going through some of the same bullying issues, but his were actually worse, because his bullying had gone online and viral. She was "all done" with this crap too. After that long chat, we, often on particularly bad days, would recite our new motto to each other: "Hurt me, don't care at all. Hurt my baby, and hold my damn wine and look out. I'm comin'." To this day, Jacqui and I are quite close. Nothing binds you like a common cause, especially one that involves kiddos. I have found that several times throughout my life, during times of horrible stress, the universe delivers a dear and long-term friend. Jacqui was and is that.

We got together to discuss how we would make things better and, quite frankly, to vent about the "Mayberry queens." Mayberry queens were perfectly dressed moms in lovely homes, with perfect families in our "perfect town." Of course, there were also lots of lovely, smart, down-to-earth, and compassionate moms. In fact, most moms were kind and helpful. The "queens" were just a tiny portion of the town, but they always let us know they ruled. Always. Their scepters were passive-aggressiveness and condescension on steroids. My son's bully's mom was one of them.

I suggested something startling to my husband and Jacqui: I wanted to start opening up about the bullying in social settings with other parents. "Let's start being authentic, open, and honest," I said. We waded into this lightly because, back in 2009, you simply did not talk about bullying. If you admitted your child was being bullied, it signaled you were a bad parent and were accusing another family of being a substandard family. It might even mean—*gasp!*—that Mayberry might not be a compassionate and kind place—*double gasp! The horror!*

In addition to getting Quinn a therapist who specialized in bullying, I started to study it as if I were writing a white paper for work. I researched bullying types, quantification of the issue in the US and in my state, best practices, the psychology of bullying, bullies' motivations, the bullied, history of bullying, treatment programs, memoirs of bullies, memoirs of the bullied, etc. Once I felt up to speed, I put my management-consulting big-girl pants on and was off to solve it with my friend.

Sadly, the conventional wisdom in these textbooks, white papers, and expert opinions was often the centuries-old "Just ignore it; the bully will get tired." Nope, no mama, it does not work that way! I decided to spend more time actually digging into the experience of those who had lived with bullying, and that is when things got interesting.

Jacqui had been studying up too. We decided to arrange meetings with the school board. Because Mayberry school administrators did not like feisty, outspoken mamas engaging in any level of badassery, they gave me a pat on the head and told me to sit down. I smiled and said, "Thank you," which really meant, *f-you. I will be back, you little toad-faced weenies. Just wait.*

I now realize my badassery sword was also being fueled by my South Side Chicago Irish DNA into a masterful and laser-focused plan to turn Mayberry into Compassionateberry. Fire!

After I was metaphorically patted on the head and told to wait, I decided I was not in the mood. So, I moved my office into the waiting area of the principal's office the next day. I loaded up my SUV and drove to my son's school. First, I brought poinsettias to the office workers (because they had been very kind to my son) and dropped them off. Next, I brought a filing cabinet filled with data I was using on a project for work and set it next to a chair in the waiting room. I brought in a TV table for my laptop and started to work.

The office workers asked me what I was doing. I replied, "Oh, I know that the principal indicated he was so terribly busy, that he would not be able to see me for three weeks, so I decided I would help out and make it easier to chat with me when he had time. I have a home office and am quite mobile. So, to better facilitate our schedules, I am making myself available right here in the waiting area. That way, whenever the principal comes or goes, he will see me, and perhaps we can just have a spontaneous meeting." Big smile, a wink, and then I took off my cute little bolero jacket and got to work in the principal's waiting area. The principal learned of my mobile office two hours later when he came out for lunch. I smiled broadly and said, "Hey, good to see you. Let me know when you have a minute."

The principal said, "Mrs. Newman, you cannot stay here."

I contradicted, "Oh, but I can." We went through another day of this, and he gave in. I told him my requirements: I needed a meeting with him, the superintendent, and the president of the school board. They agreed a week later. In that meeting, I shared my documentation, quantified known cases of bullying in Mayberry, and my theory that it was happening to many other families. They were aghast about the prevalence of bullying and "wanted to think about it." Fair, but we had now been going through this torture for over a year, and "just thinking about it" was not helpful.

At that point, I decided the urgency was just not there. Getting creative proved to be the best move. I decided to begin sharing the truth about our situation with friends and acquaintances and started talking openly with parents in every town space about bullying. Little by little, in hushed tones, folks started sharing their tales in big numbers. It was now heading toward the end of fifth grade, and we had seen some progress from the school. They installed a hall monitor, alerted key teachers. Not nearly enough.

We made it through summer and got ready for sixth grade. Quinn was still in football, and interestingly, most of the kids there were kind and inclusive. The head bully, who had mostly stopped, was still around, but other starter bullies had taken his place. Bullying really is like an infectious disease; the spread is very hard to contain. Kids typically bully because they are bored, do not understand it is wrong, have insecurities, or were bullied by a family member or other kids. It is learned behavior—we are not wired at birth for bullying; it is cultivated.

While Quinn's bullying was still omnipresent (but much more subtle now), other families started to really open up. I decided to quantify it in our schools. I took all my research and documentation and asked to present my findings at a full school board meeting. At the presentation, I opened with this: "Right now, we have one hundred known cases of severe or moderate bullying in a population of thirty-four thousand people. That exceeds the national norm by double. Also, more than one child has ideated around suicide because of the bullying." They were shocked. I was not shocked, but they were. Interesting to note that in 2010, this was a shocking statistic, but it is not at all shocking today, which makes my stomach turn.

Nevertheless, they put together a full task force, and similarly, it mobilized the community. Within one day of that presentation, dozens of families called and asked for my help. While continuing to work on Quinn's issues, Jacqui and I helped other families and became the default, antibullying ombudsmen within the school district. We helped other families frequently, and we knew we were making progress.

My friend and I were asked to work with a large group of experts designated by the governor to develop an antibullying manual for schools. We participated and enjoyed our time with a wonderful group of compassionate leaders.

From there, Jacqui and I decided we should take our research and write a manual in book form (it was Jacqui's idea). I'm glad she recommended it. We told our stories and offered practical advice that was published the next year. If it was not for Jacqui during those dark days of my son being abused, I don't know what I would have done. My husband and I were so appreciative of her because we could speak honestly and openly. She was a godsend. Make sure you find a few of those in your life. Friends with shared lived experiences are irreplaceable.

Before we finished the book, the next shoe dropped. On the first day of seventh grade, Quinn was humiliated and tortured at every turn. The lieutenant bullies put together a strategic "bullying plan" for the first day of school. The new bully leader met Quinn at the bike rack with disgusting insults as he walked into school. Next up was a group whispering and pointing in the halls (which continued throughout the day). Other bullying included putting gross things on his chair, taunting, whispering in Quinn's ear. You get the picture. By sixth period, Quinn had had all he could take. A kid came up to him and said something rude, and Quinn threw him into the lockers and said, "I can't take this anymore." This was his first day of school, for God's sake.

The vice principal, whom I had worked with on a wide variety of solutions for Quinn, was crestfallen and called me. "Marie, I am so sorry. It is like wildfire; we just cannot contain this for Quinn." He was very kind. We spoke further, but we knew it was a losing battle.

Quinn and I went home and laid down on his bed. We cried, and I whispered, "Honey, I am so sorry I haven't been able to fix this. Dad and I are going to figure this out. I promise." My husband rushed home and was fit to be tied that kids could be so cruel. We stood in our kitchen for a long embrace and started talking through the next steps.

Over a glass of wine, I blurted out, "We need to take him out of that godforsaken bully hellhole." He agreed. At the school exit meeting the next day, I sobbed and eked out, "No child should have to suffer this. It is ridiculous. We have to take this measure and take him away from the only school system he has ever known."

Now what to do about school for him? We decided to get the school to tutor him until we could find a new one. That proved challenging and, oddly, a little funny at times.

Team Newman compiled a list of schools to visit and tour. First up was a local charter school. It was twenty minutes away, only gifted kids were accepted, and it was extremely small and snooty (with a tour guide who had one of those made-up accents like a 1940s movie star. Think Moira on *Schitt's Creek*). Nope. Second, a storefront school just getting started, which was even smaller and smelled funny (and, honestly, Quinn, being a seventh-grade boy, was not the perfumiest either!). Third, a private Lutheran school ten minutes away, with newer facilities, good tech, mostly okay. Maybe? There was a lot of Christ-a-liciousness in every room, but they were very nice and welcoming. Fourth, a neighboring public school—newish, with a kind principal, a welcoming staff, and great classrooms—but it turned out we could not cross public school districts for more than one year according to state law. Not great news.

The fifth place was a weird, New Wave, experimental, no computers situation, where kids had to draw their daily feelings on an oversized pad in first period, every day. *This would mean he could potentially learn to be even more socially challenged and isolated as well as not learning computer skills? Yikes, no.* I kept on singing "The Land of the Misfit Toys" from that old Christmas special when we talked about that place. Not a chance in hell. Finally, we looked at a Catholic school, and it was an even larger bully-haven. Never. We checked others. Nothing great.

So ultimately, we decided on the Lutheran school. Quinn toured it and liked it. He started the next week. Things started out well, but we learned that singing and religious choir were full classes and took up a good chunk of the day (WTH?). In month two, there were discussions in class about the evils of homosexuality. I could not believe how conservative these folks were. In month four, the staff and school families were constantly on an anti-pro-choice rampage. Yikes.

So, we took a deep breath, went on a long four-day weekend at my sister's house in Arizona, and decided we needed a brand-new start. We decided to move. Our house sold right away, but the buyers could not move in for a while, so we had six months to pack—yay.

We moved to another suburb closer to the city and truly lived happily ever after. Or as happy as "an after" can be. Based on the antibullying book Jacqui and I wrote, I started a fulfilling national nonprofit program that implemented some wonderful programs. I was lucky enough to attend President Obama's summit on bullying and help advocate for antibullying laws nationally. It felt like our family was turning a corner; we were all finally happy—until we saw some new smoke signals on the horizon with our youngest child. If you thought the aforementioned story was a little rough, buckle up. Team Newman was in for a doozy.

LESSON: The old adage, "Nobody is coming to save us. *We* have to save us," is true. Sometimes it does have to be *you* building something from scratch to fix a tough problem.

HOW:
- When you have a thorny problem and cannot find a solution that works for you or your family, it is on you to build something from scratch to solve the problem.

- So, just do it. Research it. Open up about the problem to friends. Ask for help. Seek guidance from experts. Put your fear away. Document and journal your learnings and knowledge. Then write a plan. Yes, write down the steps. Then execute the plan.
- If you need help with your planning process, as you plan to make a change or pivot, see my "Life Made from Scratch" planning series on my website at marienewmanstudio.com. If you have a challenge that requires a social movement in your community, neighborhood, state, or nation, take a look at "Building a Movement, Made from Scratch," available on my website as well.
- And if you have specific needs with your child and bullying, please find my e-book, "When Your Child Is Bullied, Real Solutions," available on my website.

TAKEAWAYS:
- Stand up for what's right; it will often enable others to do the same.
- Sometimes, you are the one who must pick up the sticky ball in the middle of the room that nobody else wants to touch.

CHAPTER TWO

Wisdom, not character building.

A S I SHARE stories about my life, you will see a theme emerge: I don't like bullies. I won't tolerate them, but I have learned a lot from them. They taught me how to effectively address bullying and obstacles. I disagree with many experts who say being bullied is character building. It is not. Your character is built, and you are solid. What you are gaining is wisdom.

Most importantly, don't let bullies run or ruin your life. You do not have to play their game. Focus on your own game. Let them know when they have gone too far. Also learn from their motivations and behavior. There is always a lesson to be learned in those actions. Bullies are highly insecure people masquerading as fully confident (or sometimes they play the victim). Similarly, listen to your mentors, and use their experiences to inform decisions.

Interestingly, one of the most surprising lessons came from an instance of bullying post-politics for me. That unexpected message was clear: While you may leave politics, it never leaves you. An old politico friend shared, "Politics is a little like the mob. Even after you leave, everyone is always watching you and what you do, expecting supreme loyalty. Politicians are just like old Russian royalty; they bruise very easily, have skin like onions, and always expect you to protect them." Man, oh man, he was right.

Post-Congress, the wildest thing happened as I was receiving these job offers: A couple of the folks involved in hiring me indicated they had "been informed" about my political stances directly from moderate and conservative political corners. While it is hard to say who or how these petty people contacted these potential employers, I was shocked this crap lingered. I had some strong suspicions who it was and was incredibly frustrated, but I was too busy to deal with these bullies' ridiculous and petulant behavior. I chose to ignore it.

Of the offers, I chose the major nonprofit CEO role and thought that silliness was over. Fast-forward two months into my tenure, when a kind, wonderful, yet concerned donor came into my office and shared that some of her friends did not like me because I was too progressive, and a couple of political people told her I was anti-Israel, antisemitic, and anti-business. All untrue, except for the progressive part. Again, small business owner right here, with a Jewish husband. I tried to quell her fears. She seemed appeased. She was always kind and genuine to me, and I deeply appreciated her counsel. But it never ended; there were constant threats from various, isolated donors about politics, and it was exhausting. They all led back to the same tiny, isolated group who hated me.

"No words. These folks are beyond paranoid. I don't know what to do. They are ridiculously preoccupied with hating me. Honestly, I refused to believe it at first, thinking I was paranoid, but it kept coming up. I have never seen anything like it," I commiserated with an elected official, a dear friend, over a glass of wine.

She validated, "It is incredibly frustrating because these small minds always get their way, but if you call them out, even with receipts, they label you as too emotional, crazy, or a whiner. There is no winning with these bullies."

My friend had experienced similar vendettas against her by some politicians and their supporters—and, by the way, not just males. The irony here is not lost. When fragile, insecure older males call you emotional or paranoid, it usually means they are projecting. At that time, I was busy solving major structural and financial issues at the nonprofit I was working at and did not have time to address the bullies and pettiness. Unfortunately, there were specific politician bullies who trashed me and just could not move on, for reasons I still do not understand. Upon hearing this, I would just shake my head and ask, "Why are they so hate-filled, and how do they have time to attempt to make trouble?" The irony was palpable because one of these elected officials had two formal ethics complaints and an FEC investigation filed against him.

After I resigned from the nonprofit, I was consulting on some projects in DC, Chicago, and Atlanta and still talking to folks about other positions. An old friend from DC called and said, "Congresswoman, hey, it's Jeff. Do you remember me?"

"I sure do. What's up?" I said.

Jeff said several labor groups wanted me to be their nominee for a federal agency board position. They had called me the year prior about a different appointment I had declined at that time but still really cared about their issues and wanted to help. At first, I was tentative, but I learned more and thought it would be a wonderful opportunity. Well, the joy of being asked did not last long. Two elected bullies were preoccupied with hurting me and could not stop themselves. I was shocked. It was eighteen months since I lost my race, and they were still cranky? I don't understand their grudge to this day. For the record, I could never figure out why they were mad at me. A dear friend explained it like this: "Marie, your mere existence makes them nervous, and they feel threatened by you just being you." This made me think, *Am I doing something?* I thought about the last year. My opponent won by a landslide, I endorsed him, I encouraged people to vote for him, and then I shrank into the woodwork so he could do his job. I even offered to help a few times. Word moves fast in Chicago and DC political circles, and the two electeds who were inexplicably cranky with me decided to pounce and wreak havoc. These two politicians called the nominating group to tell them how upset they would be, in a threatening way, if I received this nomination and then contacted a sitting senator to whine and speak negatively about me. Just prior to this time, I'd had the audacity, as a private citizen, to actualize my free will and support two primary challengers who were opposing these two sitting incumbents in a primary. It was crystal clear that the bully politicians wanted to exact revenge against me for this "atrocity."

I thought this silliness was over, but I guessed wrong. Revenge politics is childish, yes, but it happens much more than you think. They saw this as a personal affront. *How dare I have my own life and opinions and support candidates of my choice as a private citizen? I am truly an awful human.* This is how these folks think. It is the consummate in narcissism. Ugh! After I received proof that these two elected officials were behind the hate campaign to impede my nomination, I was incredulous. The kooky part of this is that I do not have any influence in my area, and they still felt terribly angry with me for working on campaigns of my choice. They failed to understand that I was just supporting candidates I believed in—nothing more. It had nothing to do with them. I was just better aligned to their challenger's platforms. It was not some peculiar way to "hurt" them. It is striking how narcissistic they were.

At this point, I had been bullied enough. I was done, but I worried about this set of events and what it could mean for the future, if they chose to keep impeding my opportunities. I laugh so heartily when I think about these two knuckleheads because they were both in contested primaries, yet they had plenty of time to bully me for months on end. When I was a member of Congress, in a primary fight, I did not have time to play petulant bullying games. Obviously, they did.

I decided to address it. I contacted government legal counsel in DC and found out the legal/criminal/ethics ramifications for elected officials who bully, intimidate, stalk, defame, attempt to interfere in a private citizen's job prospects, or damage their reputation with professional colleagues is quite serious. It's called *abuse of power*, a criminal offense. Additionally, these actions could be considered stalking, intimidation, or defamatory on the civil side. I contacted these two knucklehead politicians and let them know I would take the higher ground for now, but I was not playing around and was done being understanding about their awful bullying behavior. I had confirmed that they had crossed a line, and I was not afraid of them. Their hate train stopped. I also realized, within a short time, if I had taken legal action, reported their behavior to the Ethics Committee or law enforcement, or publicized their behavior, I would have been acting just as retaliatory as they were. That would not be right or represent my values, so I decided I would simply feel sorry for them and walk away. Interestingly, after that, I felt immediate empathy for the depth of stress they must have felt to drive their unkind actions. I genuinely felt they must be deeply tortured to act so unjustly. I truly felt deep pity for them and let it go fully.

For bullies out there, revenge is like an addiction; you will not be satiated until you stop. So, my advice? Stop before you start. Don't become addicted to revenge. Learn from bullying. Sometimes there is a full battle, and both the bully and you are in a full-time war. This is horrible, and I recommend you set up a coffee to end it or create a truce. If they won't respond, make sure you let folks know you are being bullied and let it get back to the bully. I assure you, being known as a bully will not be what they want. In any event, do not participate in their war. Then forgive them and move on. If they want a one-sided war, let them have it. A one-sided war is weird, not satisfying, and they will burn out at some point. Your job is to keep believing in your values and rock on. Go work hard and enjoy life. Success will come.

Sometimes you just have to be hit over the head! I'm grateful to the bullies for helping me realize great opportunities and the joy that came after losing a federal job opportunity.

Home in on your passion and purpose. It will be your nirvana.

You may find a job that fulfills your passion, or perhaps you can volunteer for your passions in your free time. Closed doors simply mean there are great wide-open spaces you are being called to and you need to run to them and explore.

Either way, you got this!

Now, onto mentors. Do yourself a favor; always have a mentor. I cannot stress this enough. My mentors in advertising, management consulting, nonprofit leadership, and politics have been invaluable! Early in my career, in my twenties, I did not take enough time to build close relationships with someone older, and I wish I would have!

In my mid-thirties, I found one who was brilliant, had personality likenesses to me, and understood my perspective. He had worked with the best, brightest, and most challenging people at the very best ad agencies. His name was Neil. He was and is insightful, wise, and not preachy. We met at a midsize ad agency where I was placed in senior management.

He would frequently regale me with great advertising stories about pompous clients, overindulged account executives, hugely overconfident executives, and brilliant creatives. He really "got me," our industry, and the players. I always got along best with creatives because they usually had the best insights and found the truths in consumers' motivations, decision processes, and lives. Frequently to the dismay of a client, their creative concepts often exposed brand deficiencies or fallacies and would make the client uncomfortable. I always loved the "hitting a nerve" creative we presented. It makes you a better practitioner, and your clients learn that their product or service may need some help.

Neil was my go-to for years when I was frustrated with a client, angry with a colleague, loving my job, hating my job, starting my own business, or starting my own nonprofit.

Neil's best advice when I was feeling injustice and frustrated was this: "Let it wash over you, and don't act on it." In other words, breathe through your Irish temper tantrum, Marie, and don't eviscerate them with your tongue. Wink! Man, he does know me very well.

When my son was being bullied, I found a great therapist mentor to help our family. When Evie was transitioning, I found her older transgender mentors to help her. When it came to needing an older sister/friend/mother figure, I met someone about seven years ago, who has helped me with my family, husband, and life issues. I adore her. She shares her family's imperfections and how she "blissfully ignores" and "intensely addresses" matters and her criteria for both. So helpful.

One of my professional mentors took me to lunch about twenty years ago, right after I started my consulting business. I told her I found business development challenging. Pam's smile was unique and filled with mischief. She had dimples the size of quarters, with the twinkliest eyes, and her mere presence made me feel uplifted. She shared some great advice.

"Marie, you have two secret weapons that are not used together often, which make them very powerful," she stated, her eyes darting about the room like she was about to share a secret. "I have watched you charm clients with your wit and command of facts. But you know what? Lots of folks can do that, so understand that it is table stakes. Your secret weapons are that you are a great communicator, and you are a savant at process. You always break down hard concepts into fun and interesting language, but you are also incredibly adept with solving chaos. Further, you make it fun. You help people understand the one-two punch of communicating with the right steps and at the right time." Pam sat back and then leaned in again. "Now, do two things: Make sure you carry your secret weapons with you, and use them every day. Practice makes perfect. However, I have some future advice that will be harder to hear. You have changed jobs a lot. Always reaching for something new. You are extremely curious. But the danger with that is that you do not stick around long enough to get fully settled in and live through many cycles. With your new business in place, you must settle in. Finish what you start, lady."

She was blisteringly correct. I took it to heart and kept my business in place for fifteen years.

As we hugged goodbye that day, she said, "You know how Dorothy in *The Wizard of Oz* always possessed the ability to get home but just needed to be told? Well, you, my dear, have now been told. Go get 'em."

Ladies: know your secret weapons and use them. Know your flaws and work on them.

Have mentors. But wait, also *be one*! Over the years, I have mentored lots of folks in marketing, nonprofits, government, management consulting, and life.

I've learned from them; they've learned from me! After all, reaching back is how women have made progress. Sisters, make sure you reach back whenever you can!

LESSON: What if I was someone who did not have options after feeling the aftermath of bullying? I have thought about this broadly. While I was very lucky and had other opportunities to seek after the bullies beat down one of them, what if I did not? Guess what? You have to make your own opportunities and dedicate time to this. Don't let a bully's spite take your time and talents away. You still own both. Vendettas and revenge really are just like an addiction; if you do not stop, you will never be satiated or happy. I know one thing for sure: do not use the bullying tool of vendetta; it is very unhealthy and prevents you from building something from scratch or implementing a big pivot. See this period as a learning experience. Use your mentors when you are overwhelmed. Particularly, when it is a blend of life and professional problems. The experiences of others are why we are all here—to love, support, and serve each other. Seeking out your mentor will feel good and help you get moving.

HOW:

- Make sure, as early as your college years or early adulthood (eighteen to twenty-two), you develop mentors in your personal life, professional life, family, and other areas. It doesn't really matter when or how; just find one. The sooner you start learning from them, the easier life gets. You can find these mentors at work, industry events, online, and in your neighborhood. In short, they are everywhere.

- When you feel the most dejected, frustrated, sad, defeated, or in despair, go to your partner/best friend to get comfort. After the tears dry, go see your mentor and get the next steps started.
- Remember, you have the fortitude to stand up to a bully, and you must. The old adage, "Just ignore the bully and they'll get tired," is a big load of BS. You need to let them know they have crossed a line. You also need to reflect on what they did, why they did it, and what it means. Sometimes their cruelty was just a sign that the direction you were in was not the right one for you. Alternately, that direction may be the right one, and being bullied helped you prepare for future challenges.
- If you need help with your next pivot or solution, take a look at "A Life Pivot, Made from Scratch" on my website, marienewmanstudio.com.
- Make sure, at a certain point at work, home, with friends, and in your personal life, to mentor someone. If younger or junior people reach out, help them. *You* have a great deal to offer. And sidebar: you learn a great deal from them as well! Mentoring is good for everybody on all sides.[1]

TAKEAWAYS:
- Don't be a victim. While it is important to point out bullies, don't let being a victim of a bully define you. Learn from it and move the heck on. Take time to reflect and see if you could have done something differently.
- Don't start vendettas. They are childish and beneath you.

- You can only control your behavior, not a bully's, so choose wisely how you decide to operate.
- Find out where your passion and purpose collide, and it will empower you to find the best job for you.
- Early and at every stage, develop relationships with mentors.
- Share your knowledge and mentor young people—it will help them and you!
- Make sure you know what your secret weapons are and use them.
- Think positively and develop a new solution from scratch! It will be fulfilling and helpful to those that need it.

PART TWO

Lessons from Life Events

CHAPTER THREE

"I'm not a boy, I'm a girl, and my name is Evie."

JUST WHEN YOU think you are ready to breathe.

Coming off a huge family challenge with my oldest son and bullying, another one was dead ahead, and man, it was a doozy. My youngest child, who had always been a bubbly, funny, adventurous, and all-around fun child, had developed extreme depression and social anxiety in junior high.

At first, I thought it was because of his lingering objection to our move from another western suburb only two years prior. Our move was to create a fresh start for our oldest, but in life, for every positive action, there is always a reaction of unintended consequences. Those consequences were clear: moving affected our youngest in a deeply traumatic way. I have never felt more guilt as a mother than when I saw the crushing sorrow our youngest felt about moving.

The decision to move from Glen Ellyn to LaGrange was not impetuous; it was a slow build. The two preceding years had been a hellscape for Quinn. By contrast, Tyler, our youngest, was having the time of his life. On the surface, the Newmans had the world by the proverbial tail. Deciding to move was truly a Sophie's choice.

Being very decisive and living with unusually strong clarity is one of my hallmarks, so the angst associated with the move was new territory for me. The decision was fraught with second-guessing and murkiness. Signs are something I always pay very close attention to. Here's why: When I was in college and had just been dumped by a long-term boyfriend, I was incredibly busy feeling sorry for myself (like it was a full-time job with loads of overtime). I was sitting head in hands on the steps of the library and thinking, *Why isn't God sending me the answer? I have been thanking Him for years, I go to church, so I deserve an answer.* Suddenly, a friend of mine, known for her candor and fabulous writing skills, sat next to me and told me an old joke.

"A man capsized in the ocean, hanging onto a piece of driftwood and praying hard that God would save him. His faith held strong. On the first day, a small rowboat came by, and a man told him to come aboard. The drowning man said, 'No, God will save me.' Second day, a helicopter throws a life preserver out, and the man says, 'I'm good, waiting for God to come.' Third day, a barge comes and sends a Navy SEAL to rescue. The drowning man screams, 'God is coming. You do not have to worry about me,' to which the SEAL said, 'I don't know, dude, I think this is the third time God brought you a damn opportunity. Who do you think sent all of these options to you?' The man thought for a minute and said, 'Oh.'"

I looked up and smiled. At twenty, I figured out that you have to understand the signs and know you are presented with opportunities to solve your own problems; God/Mother Nature/the Universe does not actually solve your problems. You have to solve your own problems by finding your own opportunities.

As the challenge for Quinn brewed and we were thinking about whether to move, we literally got a note in our mailbox offering a fair and competitive price in the middle of a housing crisis and housing bust nationally (2011). It was our sign. We moved.

Tyler was devastated. On a Sunday night, we told the kids, "Pumpkins, you know how sometimes there are things adults decide on that are hard to understand at first but make sense later? I think we have some news like that now."

Both kids' eyes narrowed, and they visibly took a deep gulp. "After months of thought, Mom and I have decided to move to LaGrange," Jim slowly offered.

"What?" Tyler screamed. Quinn sat in disbelief, neither sad nor happy. We explained, cajoled, overempathized, and desperately helped them understand that a fresh start was needed. Tyler cried for hours and finally fell asleep.

Fast-forward to our first few weeks in our new home in LaGrange, and it was desolate for them. There were not a lot of summer activities or park district events, so meeting other kids was really rough. One night, I caught Tyler sitting in the dark in his room with his stuffed animals, weeping and repeating, "I have no friends left. I'm all alone. This is awful." It would be two whole months until school started. Tyler cried a good bit at night. We did our best to have activities every day.

When school started, I really pushed Tyler to go to friends' houses and invite them to ours. After constant convincing, he made a nice group of friends, played football, and by the end of fifth grade seemed relatively happy. Things were pretty good for about a year.

Then things took a turn in late sixth grade. It was a slow progression but gradually became obvious. In February that year, he developed migraines, and they were quite something. When these bombs struck his head, he had to be in complete darkness and silence after downing Advil and keeping a cold cloth on his head. Sometimes, I would hold him and lay on his bed for hours while he wept. Doctors prescribed medication that helped a bit, but not a lot. Other than the migraines, nothing else was pronounced until the summer after sixth grade. He seemed to be getting in fights with his friends more than ever before, often saying, "Mom, they just don't understand anything. They don't get me."

Then, he started isolating in the middle of seventh grade. Fewer friends called. Fewer outings. By the end of seventh grade, he was down to just a few friends. He also constantly lashed out at the smallest of issues. That's the wrong sandwich, the computer was not working fast enough, and he hated his shirts. Always something. He spent hours in his room alone. It was clear he was in a full depression. Depression and anxiety run in both families. I knew it. I researched therapists, conditions, and remedies. We tried several therapists and therapeutic groups over eighteen months. *Nine* to be exact. They all said the same thing. Your son absolutely will not open up, and I cannot make him. The last therapist said, "Marie, he is deeply angry and in intense pain; I suggest trying group therapy." We did.

We thought we had tried everything: therapy, medication, programs, activities, camps, new friends, and interesting vacations and places. I was always researching new options. His sadness, rage, and desolation seemed to only worsen with every solution, and it was not until later that we saw how much more complex it was. His anger was growing and scaring me a bit. At night, I would pray for a sign, a hint, a clue—anything that might help us solve this.

On the day before his eighth-grade graduation, we decided to take him out for burgers and bowling. It was mid-afternoon on a beautiful May day, and my husband had just gotten into an argument with Tyler about him isolating, being rude, and not helping with anything around the house. I finally said, "I just don't know what to say anymore, Tyler. We are just beyond exasperated, exhausted with you. You have got to let us help you; go take some time and think about this." He charged upstairs.

A couple hours later, he tentatively came downstairs with his head hung low and said with tears in his eyes, "Uh, Mom, Dad, look, I know I can be an ass, and I'm a huge hassle. I get it. Really, I think there are only two things I can think of that will fix it."

Inhaling deeply, I said, "What?" I was irritated, predicting he would say, "I will try a little harder" or something similar.

Tyler said, "Well . . . I think I can either run away or kill myself." *Boom.* The world stopped. That serrated blade of a sentence just ripped through me.

My husband and I leaped to our feet, grabbed him, and enveloped him in an extended, tight hug. "Oh my God, neither are good ideas, neither! Oh my God. Oh my God." It was not what I expected. Kids exaggerate all the time. This was not a hyperbole from Tyler. He was fourteen but had been in a deep depression that seemed never-ending. To make it worse, on that day, I felt like he was not "trying" hard enough. I felt like the worst mother on the planet.

That night, we stayed with him wherever he went. Most of the night, I researched facilities, hospitals, or outpatient programs that would take him immediately. Jim and I talked for hours and decided we would have him go through graduation that following night and then admit him the next day to a well-suited program to address adolescent depression via an outpatient program. We took turns "sleeping" in his bedroom and made sure he did not hurt himself that night, but we really did not sleep at all.

Our family zombied our way through the graduation ceremony and got ice cream. We all squeezed into a booth at our favorite ice-cream place and sat there very quietly. I had to work really hard to hold back my tears. I tried to talk about how this new outpatient place was "all the rage," "had the answers," and "will really help," and we kept saying, "We are so proud of you for graduating and agreeing to get help. We love you so much."

What we didn't know is that while this day program was very helpful with his depression challenge, we found out that the depression was just a symptom of another issue. My youngest child, who at birth was my son, Tyler, was not living an authentic and comfortable life. Within days of enrolling him into a specialized eight-week, all-day therapy program that specialized in anxiety and depression for adolescents, Tyler (at the time) made a huge discovery. He looked up from his spaghetti as I asked, "How did things go today, honey?"

"Mom, I figured it out." Long pause. "I'm not a boy, I'm a girl, and my name is Evie. Well, actually, I think I'm gender-fluid. I think that is the term. But mostly, I'm a girl."

I was literally thrilled. I threw my hands up, cheered her, leaped to her, hugged her, and said, "I'm so proud of you."

And, in true Evie style, she said, "Okay, Mom, settle down now. Don't get nuts."

From there, it was to be a long and treacherous road, but the hardest part was knowing she had been inauthentic with herself and everyone for years. She must have been so scared. It still levels me when I think about it. This set of events would be a signal for my role in the future. My smoke signals in this instance were to educate and advocate. I did. Jim and I found the wonderful Lurie Children's Hospital program for gender development, and our family became active with that community of 100 or so families. We became advocates and spokespeople. Evie found friends and activities. We will forever hold Lurie and its marvelous doctors, therapists, and staff in our hearts as the most credentialed and compassionate angels we have ever met. I love them with my whole heart.

I have told that story many times since that day in 2014, usually in the context of discussing authenticity. In my humble opinion, I truly believe authenticity is the most important thing for humans. Without it, there is no path to happiness, which was really at the base of Evie's challenge, we came to find out.

An interesting finding as we embarked on our journey with this community of families with transgender kids is that, like all families, dynamics around this topic are quite diverse. At our first monthly Lurie family community meeting, the kids went into one area to hang out, play games, and chat. The parents went into another room to do group chatting (literally a disguise for group therapy). The room was a study in body language to say the least. Parents who were hesitant or not "all in" about their child transitioning or being nonbinary were pushed back from the table with hands clasped in their lap, sitting solemnly. The parents who were all in, wanting to learn more and hear folks' stories, were leaning in, watching, and hanging on every word. We started with icebreakers, moderated by the program staff. They were lovebugs and normalized all our feelings no matter what we said. It was like a warm, sunshiny hug every time we were there.

I distinctly remember one of the parent couples as a vivid tutorial in "don't judge a book by its cover." The mother was an artist with colorful clothes on, a warm smile, and a friendly attitude. I thought for sure she would be very supportive. The father was a police officer with tattoos, reserved but very engaged, and he listened intently. We came to learn that Artist Mom sort of was "not buying it," and Tattoo Dad was very "proud and ready to support." Pleasant surprise! In fact, the police officer was incredibly empathetic and understood a great deal about transgender kids because he had helped many when they were homeless and victims of crimes over the years. These teens are often victimized in our society, and it is beyond heartbreaking. He was lovely and kind. Mom stayed cranky for weeks and then gradually came to accept her daughter's new identity. Note to self: don't start with a disposition based on how someone presents.

Another couple was more like Jim and me, both supportive, one spouse ready, willing, and at the starting gate, and the other working their way onto the field tentatively, but still very supportive. I was all in, like the kid in the front row of class constantly raising her hand with questions and answers. Jim was supportive but having trouble transitioning from a dad who had coached his son's baseball team to one who had a daughter he had very little in common with, who now had a new identity. The couple similar to us was at about the same phase we were, and it helped so much. I bought a gazillion books, watched videos and documentaries, and met with experts. Jim read all I gave him and worked hard. It was helpful to have some parents we could relate to and especially helpful for Jim to have someone he could relate to authentically as a dad.

Each month we met with this group, we would bring a tip or lesson we discovered that would help other families. The second month, I offered our new practice at home called "the pronoun jar." Our family created this so we could all retrain our brains to use Evie's correct name and pronouns. Every time one of us used her old name (referred to as dead-naming) or an incorrect pronoun when referring to her, we had to put a dollar in the jar. Early days, Evie easily made twenty to thirty dollars per week. We would laugh, and it helped us as a family to keep it light and tight. The family therapy group now uses that as part of their approach.

Living authentically is important for everyone, to be sure, but for those who have folks who have recently transitioned from their former gender to a new gender, there are many new things to learn. In fact, for me and most parents of transgender kids or siblings of transgender loved ones, it becomes a new, overwhelming job. Case in point, literally within one week of Evie coming out, I put my business on hiatus for three months so I could research how to support her, take care of her, identify health-care partners, and adjust my brain.

A mentor in the transgender family space, whom I had serendipitously met two years prior to Evie's announcement, helped me more than she will ever know. Thank you, Debbie! As with any new adventure, have a mentor, find a community, and read as much as you can. I was lucky; I was able to stop working for a few months, and not everyone can do that. So, if you find yourself in that spot, get help, don't be bashful, ask friends and family to help you learn, and find resources to help your loved one.

Now, one note, a tough reality I share with all parents who ask for my counsel in helping their child with their transition, is a hard one to hear for parents newly aware of their child's authenticity. It is heart-wrenching. About a month after you, as a parent, become settled into this new truth, you will fully fall apart, and I will tell you why (it is not because you do not want your child's new authenticity; it is something very different).

This happened to me. Six weeks after Evie announced her identity, I had just finished getting her health-care routine set up and finalized her city social groups schedule, and it hit me like an overwhelming Category-5 hurricane. One morning after breakfast, Evie had just gone upstairs to play video games, and I burst into tears out of nowhere. Tyler was gone. Tyler was, effectively, dead. Of course, I am thrilled that Evie was finally happy and living authentically, more than you can imagine, but my sweet baby, Tyler, the boy I had given birth to fourteen years prior, was completely gone. On that day, the velocity of this notion hit me all at once. As I stood in the kitchen, I felt it like a brick to my chest. To break my fall, I clutched the sink, coughed out an ugly cry, and then fell to my knees. I wept like I had never wept before. Tyler was gone, completely. I did not want Evie to see me crying, so I splashed cold water on my face and yelled upstairs, "Hey, pumpkin, I have some errands to run. I'll be back a little later." I rushed out the door and started crying uncontrollably. Intuitively, I knew I had to let it out. I just could not get over the finality of it. It was just like mourning a child's death, but interestingly, giving birth at the same time. After gaining a little composure, I drove to a park in the next suburb over and cried in my car for an hour; then I got out. Seated on a corner bench in the park, I stared intensely at kids playing a block away and thought about how I would never see Tyler again. I wallowed in my grief for another hour.

I worked my way back to a better emotional space by remembering . . . I have a daughter. I always wanted a daughter, and this will be a wonderful, fresh start. It took some time. I went home and read more about how to relearn pronouns, understand hormone therapy, find resources for Evie, etc. I rebounded over a period of days and never looked back. But, parents and families, you will have a day of mourning. *Know that.* Brace for it, work it out, and then thank your many blessings for this new start. Life is better with authenticity—believe me!

Life definitely never played out the way I planned. As the youngest of four in a middle-class family in middle America, I assumed I would go to college, meet a brilliant and gorgeous man, and then marry him. Next, have an amazing marriage, with a perfectly traditional family with three children, be a CEO of something, solve a pressing issue, like homelessness in the US, oh, and, of course, have a beautiful home. And, *ooh*, yes, be thin and in shape my whole life.

Wah-wah! Bzzzzzt (buzzer sound). Wrong. All of it.

While it was not that fairy tale at all, in the quirkiest and most unexpected ways, it was, simply, much more. And it has been beautiful in the way the worn and ragged Velveteen Rabbit was in the story—because it is "real" and authentic.

God has always had a strong sense of humor with me. In fact, he likes to help me understand life with very blunt interventions, practical jokes, and pranks designed to facilitate understanding and be excruciatingly clear with me. Generally, these demonstrations force me to stop walking through fire and redirect myself. I learned to listen over time, but it took me a while. Sometimes it simply means I need to learn something new and build something from scratch.

Sometimes, the universe, God, or whatever you believe in pushes you down a path that you did not think you needed to go down, but curiously, it brings you everything you wanted, so trust that blueprint. When Mother Nature puts up barriers and forces you down a path you had no interest in or did not think you could manage, pay attention—because it will bring you all that you need *and* all that you wanted.

But, because I can be pretty dense and stubborn, God regularly sprinkles in "teachable moments" such as dealing with the traumatizing bullying of my first child (Quinn) for years, helping my second child transition from male to female (Evie), dealing with mental health challenges in my family for decades (and not always with enough empathy, if I'm being honest), winning a congressional election, becoming a congresswoman, living through a manufactured scandal, losing lifelong friends, and finally, losing an election in a full-on landslide. Oh, and dealing with impostor syndrome at every turn. So, if I had to name my fairy-tale life book, it would be *Living Life on Opposite Day*.

Signs are our best friends. Evie's transition was a sign that my daughter needed help, but it was also a sign that our family needed to reconnect. Signs become more important as we age, see them, listen to them, and act on them.

I became a spokesperson and advocate for the gender development organization Evie benefited from, and I continue to work with them. Similarly, whenever I get a call about a child transitioning—and a family needs help—I help. I even have a kit to send to the family. Follow the signs when you are needed.

LESSON: When life sends you a huge challenge, it is much more than just "God does not give you more than you can handle." The universe is telling you that you need to learn, grow, and help. Sometimes, it means putting life on hold to help a child, loved one, or friend, and maybe even yourself.

HOW:
- When a challenge comes along, you have no experience with it, and it hurls from out of the blue, take a deep breath. It's a lot. Make sure you recognize it is a big deal and a mountain to climb, but remember the first step is the hardest. In the case of a loved one transitioning, take those first steps quickly:
- Tell your child you love and accept them, and ask them what they need.
- Make sure your child's mental health is cared for; coming out and transitioning will likely be the hardest thing they ever do. Call a therapist or health-care provider to support their emotional health.
- Start researching what to do right away. A shortcut is my "Supporting Your Transgender Child, Life Made from Scratch Planning Guide," available on my website. There are lots of great resources out there.
- Get started right away, even if it's a small step. It is just like walking up a mountain: take one step at a time, but don't ever stop. Make sure you follow the steps in my planning guide or best practices from experts.

TAKEAWAYS:
- When signs make it clear that your challenge is undeniable, it must be addressed, you must teach yourself how to do it, and you must fully own it. Go ahead and own it!
- Take the time to learn about the issue you're facing, learn how to manage it, and do it with gusto!
- If you are in the early days of a community movement or cause, assemble your partners and coalitions first, always. Strength in numbers!
- Bring humor to every challenge; it helps even if it hurts a little.
- Accept, embrace, and accomplish!

CHAPTER FOUR

It Was Not a Shameful Act

LIFE COMES AT you fast, and certain events have more impact than others. My personal abortion story shaped my worldview at a very young age. It was likely my very first high-octane life fire. A surprise pregnancy at nineteen is not something any young woman just out of high school is ready for. But I came from a devout Catholic, middle-class, Midwestern family that typically reacted with shame in these types of situations. It wasn't that my family shamed me; I just felt it would be discerned that way.

It was my perception.

Two weeks before my decision to abort, I reflected deeply on my family and childhood memories, which helped me understand with clarity what was best. Revisiting pivotal moments helped make my decision clear. I thought about everything: My father's job loss at an early age and how it affected me. Remembering and admitting (to nobody except myself) that I did not like babysitting at all and candidly (although, in an Irish Catholic community, you are verboten to say it), I did not really enjoy kids. Those admissions were simply not shared in my ruby-red conservative suburb growing up.

During that time, I contemplated my mother's eighties-sitcom-like concept of being a homemaker (bridge, golf, gourmet club, and cooking every meal) and developed a distinct curiosity of my mother's complete lack of interest in a career. It was a skewed perception because I did not understand her and truthfully never asked her about it. It was not a lack of ambition; she simply liked homemaking. Having a baby was in direct conflict with my huge plans to be an executive responsible for ending homelessness and my FOMO (fear of missing out). These were all factors in my decision to have an abortion, but it also revealed the tensions with my family that were precursors and signs of struggles to come. I was taught to believe that abortion was a shameful act. It was murder. I did not agree but still felt ashamed.

This was a situation where I found the fire, and the fire found me. I had sex and did not expect it to change my life, but it did.

The tussle with myself was painful. The possibility of losing the hard-won achievements at college was a factor. But, also, if I'm being one-hundred-percent honest, another factor was a clear and compelling desire to party, have adventures, and have a good time. Yup, I said it. Brutal honesty with myself made it convincingly clear: I still wanted to have fun, have a career, and "not just be a mom." Finally, my decision to pursue my life the way I wanted became clear as day. An abortion is not a shameful act.

Yet I kept it an iron-clad secret. It would take another twenty years for me to tell my closest friends or sisters. That decision was transformative and a clear sign of other tough decisions ahead. I learned that I am capable of very tough decisions and that my opinion matters. I am also capable of walking through fire and building my own solutions.

On the morning of my abortion, I vividly recall that the room was freezing. Alone and mortified, with heavy notes of terror and guilt, I sat wearing one of those awkward patient gowns that ties in the back. In a sterile room, I shivered while looking at all the aluminum tables with shiny equipment. It all felt industrial, not medical. I felt tears running down my face, but my mind was racing so fast, I did not know I was crying. As I laid on the clinic bed, I kept replaying my decision, every angle, every discussion, and kept coming to the same place—this is so hard, but inescapably the right thing to do.

In the year prior, I had been happily dating a very nice young man in college who was kind, loving, very smart, and adorable. I was joyful and having late night/drinking/being silly/working hard college fun, the fun I should be having. It was the beginning of my sophomore year, and my dorm was filled with funny, smart folks from all over, and I loved getting to know all of them.

My kind and sweet boyfriend had just transferred to another university, and I felt like I had the world by the tail. Even though he was only an hour away, I enjoyed that little separation of time and space from him. I had great friends, loved my studies, and was still close to my friends from home.

That all came to a screeching halt when I realized I was late. My period was like a clock on a computer. Every twenty-nine days, boom, five days long. No variation. Until that day in October. The first few days of being late, I really did not give it a thought.

After a week, I became nervous.

At twelve days, I told a close friend. On day fourteen, I knocked on Barb's door three doors down and started crying. We sat down on her bed and devised a plan. The plan was perfected during a walk to the drugstore. "Let's go to the drugstore on Water Street. It's farther away but safer," Barb said. "I will stand in front of you as you pick out the pregnancy test from the shelf and shield you at the counter so nobody will see what you are buying." I felt immense appreciation, hugging her tightly as I walked out the door of the store.

Later, when we got back to the dorm, we went to the least crowded bathroom, and she stood guard by the door, telling people I was sick and to go to another floor.

"Goddamn it!" I shrieked, looking at the test in disbelief. I dissolved into tears.

Barb came running in. "Let me guess, it's positive." She fell to the floor with me. Barb understood unexpected health challenges intimately. When she was younger, she had a childhood disease that was life-changing, and she was beyond empathetic. An absolute saint. We stared at it for a while, and then Barb grabbed some tissues and offered, "Let's go get some bad coffee in the cafeteria and figure this out."

By the time we sat in the dimly lit corner of the cafeteria, at an old, 1960s-style, nondescript, tile-surfaced lunch table, my head was exploding with contradictory thoughts. Being very Catholic at the time, I was disgusted and disappointed with myself. *My parents will hate me and never forgive me. What will Adam, my incredibly kind boyfriend, say? What will my friends say?* Then it struck me. *I'm obsessing over what everyone else thinks.*

As if reading my mind, Barb said, "It does not matter what anyone else thinks; it is only important what you and Adam want. Block out that other crap."

My problem was that I did not know what to think. I honestly had never thought about having babies before. *Do I want kids? Do I not want kids? Do I want a career and kids? Do I just want a career?* Jesus. I had no idea. "I'm going to call Adam as soon as I can stop crying."

Two hours later, I called him in my room while my roommate was out. "Oh, hons," he said in his super-adorable Wisconsin way. "That is tough news. What are you thinking?" I stayed quiet. "Whatever you want," he encouraged.

I finally blurted out, "I don't think I'm ready for a baby. I have no idea how to be a mom. I am so damn scared; I cannot see straight."

He was loving and said, "Do you want me to hop on a bus and come tonight? I can blow off class tomorrow and stay until Tuesday morning." He took it the way I thought he would. Adam was kind, supportive, lovely. But I knew he was feeling the same way. He was scared, not interested in being a parent, but did not say either way. The fact that he did not say, "Please, let's keep the pregnancy and make a go of it" said it all. I was glad, and it was all I needed to know.

Ultimately, over the following two weeks, we decided to have the abortion. I cried and cried, hoping it was somehow untrue. Test after test said otherwise. I was pregnant and having an abortion.

Adam made the arrangements at a clinic on campus. He went with me and held my hand.

The middle-aged nurse with blond curls and wise eyes touched my shoulder and said, "It's time, honey." The doctor was in his early fifties. He had knowing eyes. Respectfully and in a clear voice, he said, "You understand what we are doing here, Marie, yes?"

"I do," I managed.

"We'll get started then. You will feel a pinch and some pressure throughout." And that was when I literally checked out of my body, and honestly, I do not recall much at all until I was in the recovery room. That room was warmer, softer, with a blanket. Adam came in and touched my forehead, saying, "You did great, hons."

All I remember after that was sitting in the dorm room, making soup in the hot pot, and watching TV.

In the blurry weeks that followed, I worked hard to forget it. That did not work. I thought about it incessantly. The enormity of it would catch me by surprise in the oddest places. In the line at the library, talking to a friend from class, I would drift off and start crying. I told no one for years, except one priest the following spring in my junior year.

The thought of going to confession at a large contemporary church on campus was something that hounded me for months. Every time I passed by the building, I felt a palpable tug to go inside. At that time, I was still pretty faithful to Catholicism, went to church every week, and was perpetually feeling guilty about the abortion.

On a bright, sunny Saturday morning, I walked up the steps and stood in the cavernous but tranquil reception area of the sleek and modern church. A kind woman in a cardigan approached and simply said, "Hello." I could tell she saw my wet eyes. "What is it, dear?"

Sheepishly, I asked, "Is Father offering confessions at this time?"

"Let me see," she offered in a comforting and knowing way.

I settled into a pew in the front of the church where the confession signs were placed. This was much better than when I was a little girl. Dear Lord, those awful Gothic confessional boxes were dark wood, musty, and looked like where you would get tortured or worse.

This Catholic church was modern, with comfy pews and no confessionals. The priest emerged from the altar door and saw me. He was youngish, maybe thirty-five, with glasses and a slight smile. "Hi, I'm Father Pete."

"Hi, I'm Marie," I said through tears. It still makes me cry when I think about this exchange, but not for the reasons you think.

"I can tell you are carrying a very heavy load. Can I help you with that?" Father Pete chirped. The waterfall of tears began, filled with gasps, ugly crying, and hands on my mouth as if to silence myself. He put his finger up to signal "just one minute," picked up tissues from the altar, and offered them.

After I finished, he took a deep breath and nodded. "It sounds like you are looking for absolution." I looked up slightly, but not all the way up, sort of like a child who realized they may not be in big trouble but will get a brief lecture. Turns out, it was not even a lecture, more like life advice. "God loves you and wants you to have a full life. Return his love by making sure you take care of yourself and others and think about your future," he imparted like a burning bush. He put his hand on my forehead and gave me a formal absolution. I remember hugging him, and he was slightly uncomfortable. I promised I would take his sage words to heart.

Walking out, I felt lighter.

My boyfriend and I had amicably broken up months before. Leaving the church, I felt the need to reach out to him, but instead, I ran back to my apartment to seek the safety of my roommates. While I did not tell anyone at that time, I was buoyed by simply being around my roommates. They sensed something, but we just had a good time watching movies. No judgment, no prying, just smiles, easy quiet, and simply being present. I was grateful.

From that point on, I learned a great lesson: my future is both in the years to come and right now. You build your future from scratch every day, so remember that you need to blend in your life now and in the future. This episode in my life allowed me to recognize that I will always be making hard decisions, and I need to think about reality, the things I can change, the things I cannot change, such as history, and how I built from there.

What I really learned about myself was that I wanted a career, I wanted to have impact, and I could do so if I put my nose to the grindstone. From there, I concentrated on building a career—and I did.

LESSON: Listening to yourself and trusting yourself, particularly when you are young, is very hard. Often, we think we know everything, but we simultaneously know we do not. We all make choices, good and bad. I have made lots of bad choices, but I definitely learned from each and every one of them. I was always aware when I was making a bad choice: skipping class, calling in sick when I was not, staying with bad boys, spending too much money, drinking too much. Those were all clearly not good choices. I had no frame of reference on big choices; I really had to rely on playing out scenarios of the future in my head. I learned this skill when I went to college and still today run the scenarios through before making a decision.

HOW:
- Making a big decision when you are young is tricky, so make sure you run through all the possible options several times.
- Know that when you make a decision, some will cheer for you, and some will be angry. Be ready for both.
- This wise phrase for young people is absolutely true: "Don't solve a temporary problem with a permanent solution, if you can avoid it." Look at step-by-step solutions that will be a series of temporary solutions. In the case of being pregnant,

there are lots of choices, but make sure you have the life you want to live, not the life someone wants or expects you to live.
- Life solutions are for you, so get input from several, but remember it is your life, so you are the decider.
- After the decision and implementation of the course of action, have a plan ready.
- In my case, I knew an abortion and not making any further commitments to my boyfriend was correct. Beyond that, I took it day by day.

TAKEAWAYS:
- Don't let feelings of shame dominate your decision-making. Remove the notion of shame and look at the facts.
- Play out the scenarios in your head. *If I take this action, what will be the reaction? Or if I take a different action, what will happen?* Some call it critical thinking; others call it strategic. We all do this in some form or fashion.
- Take the time you need (whenever possible, take days or weeks, not just hours, with big decisions). It allows you to play out all the scenarios, take advice from others who have been there, and let it all marinate.

CHAPTER FIVE

I Was Curly-Haired and Laughing A Lot

IT TURNS OUT that being yourself is a recipe for being underestimated as a young woman in your twenties. Through a whole series of life events, I learned early in my career that being a curly-haired, enthusiastic young woman who laughs easily is the formula to not be taken seriously at work. In my mind, the obvious antidote was to cut my hair ridiculously short. I mean, we are talking two centimeters around most of my head with a two-inch bang situation and some gel. This assured no curls could poke out and be themselves in any way. Okay, and teach yourself to stop laughing so much—yes, very late eighties/early nineties of me. Also important, I thought, *I should* only *concentrate on my career for several years.* So of course, I did just that!

During that time, men were much more handsy, and I remember finding it irritating, yet somehow expected and weirdly . . . acceptable? Lordy, things were screwed up then.

After college, I remember starting out with a job in the industry I loved: advertising. It was thrilling to be learning so much, so young. My first ad agency was downtown on Michigan Avenue in Chicago in a high-rise office with fancy furniture—wide-open conference rooms with enormous mahogany tables and overstuffed couches. Add to that mix coworkers who were outsized yet exciting characters, abounding in every direction, and you had the recipe for a very cool new career.

Working in advertising in the late 1980s, one either worked on Madison Avenue (NYC) or Michigan Avenue (Chicago), or one simply did not really work in advertising at all. That remained true for a decade, until those same brilliant and creative folks who built those two hubs went onto smaller, but now incredibly respected, agencies and built empires in markets like Seattle, San Francisco, Denver, Milwaukee, and many more. Love that. Life made from scratch, yes?

Walking from the train every day, I would look up and see the buildings touch the sky and hordes of people rushing in syncopation as if it were choreographed every morning for my delight. I loved the rush, the sounds, the gleaming skyscrapers, the coffee shops, doormen, cabbies, all of it. The city made me feel alive, and I was truly in love with everything about it. And to this day, nothing picks up my mood more than walking in the city on a weekday. But I also learned early on that misogyny and mansplaining came with the territory, and as a result, experiencing impostor syndrome regularly was my new hobby. Fun!

Distinctly, I recollect one of the first times I was brought down, not just a rung or two but to the bottom of the ladder.

A few months into my first job at a top ad agency, I felt like I was on top of the world. Tanned, wearing a bright-green peplum cotton dress with high-as-the-sky heels, I had a meeting with a super-cute magazine rep who wanted me to buy space in his magazine for my car client. A new, first-of-its-kind car brand, Acura, was my new client, and I was honored to work on it. While it was not my first meeting like this, it was with a very important magazine, and the rep was a dashing sales guy. Tall, olive skin, piercing blue-green eyes, and a great suit with a wide tie large enough to act as a safety net for a circus act. Men's clothing in the nineties epitomized boxiness. Ties were big and square, suits were big and square, and shoes were giant rectangles.

It was late summer, and Jake entered the reception area. I came over to him with my hand extended. I just about melted into my shoes. Working hard not to look dazzled, I abruptly said, "I'm in a hurry and need to get a recommendation to my client, so let's go back. You said your name was Jake, right?" This was my weird way of taking control.

"The creative work your team is doing on Acura, Montgomery Ward, and Rust Oleum is so fresh," he shared with me, as if I were a senior person. I chuckled in my head.

Once we got through the gobbledygook—Where did you go to college? How did you land here? What is your next move? Love your brand, etc.—we started to chat seriously about a full spread in his publication. A full spread in a magazine at that time was a huge and expensive move. "Acura models are so sexy; you guys need a really sexy move here." Assessing that meeting in the rearview mirror, it was typical agency chatter at the time, but it now seems extra cheesy with a side of stupid. That said, Jake was not wrong. He went on and on, mostly because he would earn a whopper of a commission if he successfully landed this sale. He cajoled, flirted, played hard to get, ran an urgency play, saying, "I am running out of these spots, so you will need to really move on this," and added lots of twinkly-eyed intensity as he leaned in and said, "Hey, this was so fun. Do you want to go with me to the Cubs game tomorrow night?"

I smiled, while my knees shook underneath the desk. On one hand, he was adorable and seemed fun. On the other hand, it might be unprofessional. Wait, it really would not be a date; it would be a rep taking out a client, right? Hmmm. What do I say here? I managed, "Let me see what is going on tomorrow. Not sure I'm open" (a big fat lie). He shot me a wink.

Clearly, he was a sales guy. Clearly, I knew what he was doing. Clearly, I had heard about his reputation. So, what do I do? I asked Delilah, the office guru and my good friend.

Delilah, a tall, acerbically funny redhead who seemed very worldly to me, had a long-term boyfriend. She could make me cry laughing with just a look, and I just thought she was the absolute best. She spit out her Coke and laughed out loud. "That guy—are you kidding, Marie? Name someone he has not slept with on Michigan Ave! C'mon, he will do whatever it takes to get a sale. Yeah, sure, go if you love Cubs games. But know two things: he will make a move *and* will keep flirting until he gets the order for his pub."

I knew she was right, but he was just . . . so cute. I also thought the spread was genuinely a good idea, for real. Running it by my boss seemed like the best next step. Terry, a curmudgeonly charming middle-aged man with a sharply realistic outlook, said, "Your idea is solid, run the numbers, and see if we can do it. But Marie, watch out for that guy. He is trouble." Ugh. It is now on me.

Impetuously (a theme I was not unfamiliar with in my life), I called Jake and confirmed I was free and would love to join him.

We met at the iconic Wrigley Field. I felt so important. Not knowing if this was a date, a business outing, or something in between, I was ready. Cute skirt and top? Check. Expensive perfume I could not afford? Check. Walking up to him, a little late, with a huge smile? Check. Jake started out as the consummate gentleman. Waiting on me hand and foot with concessions, draping his suit jacket on my shoulders when it got chilly, and walking me to my door.

Still not understanding what we had here, I turned to him and started to say thank you, and he planted a kiss—not just any kiss but one I actually remember many decades later. He asked if he could come up. Again, impetuously, I said yes. He did stay the night, and I did regret it, but I was fully infatuated. I let things get out of hand. *Crap, that was dumb*, I thought as I said goodbye to him in my doorway.

I would be late getting into the office, and my boss met me in the reception area as I was walking in. "Hey, the client does want to do that four-color spread. Go make it happen, kiddo!"

I was thrilled. "Will do, thanks. Sounds good!"

I let all of twelve minutes go by and then called Jake. He said, "Cool, so good to hear. I will get the paperwork to you before noon.

Thanks. Great to do this deal with you." He hung up.

I stared at my huge fancy desk phone. "Do this deal?" What did that mean?

Delilah and Terry, right again. He was blowing me off, but he got "the deal." I got the paperwork. He shook my hand. We parted and never saw each other again. He got what he wanted. On some level, so did I, I suppose. But his was a transaction. Gotta tell ya, some version (without involving sex) of this happened a few more times while I worked at ad agencies. Sometimes, I'm just thick. I finally learned in my late twenties that business is transactional.

Another time, a couple of years later, at a different ad agency with a different boss, I started a transactional situation, but I ended it. He was another middle-aged guy, and he made me feel small and not worthy. But this time, I took control.

I could see just a tiny bit of a large dark steel corner of the Hancock building out my window as my boss sauntered over and looked over my shoulder at a media analysis I had just completed. Most of the women in my department thought Mike was very attractive. He was oddly close to me; I could smell his deodorant—a weird powder/musk thing going on. He then decided to ask a couple of questions and offered to help me make the charts on my screen better for my report.

Before I could answer, he sidled up behind where I was sitting and wrapped his arms around my shoulders from behind to access the computer keyboard and proceeded to type in some changes to my chart. I was literally boxed in with his head hovering over my shoulder and his arms around my arms stretched onto the keyboard, clicking away. He said something like, "Hey, good try here, but—" But I really could not even hear him. I froze and let him finish. It was 7 p.m., and we were the only two people in the office. I continued to stare at the steel corner of the building as if it were centering me and keeping me safe from truly understanding how violated I felt. After he made the changes on my computer, he rubbed my back and said, "Let me know if you need anything else" sort of suggestively. He lingered. I stood up abruptly and told him I had to catch my bus. I never stayed late again unless someone else was there. I made it very clear to Mr. Handsy von Handsenstein, there was no transaction here.

Mansplaining sets my hair on fire. I'm not going to even sugarcoat it. I get especially livid when *women* say, as an excuse for mansplaining men, "Oh, I don't think he is even aware he is doing it." I. DON'T. FLIPPING. CARE.

For all of time, men have done this. One of the clearest and most triggering cases of mansplaining I remember was years after the Mr. Handsy incident. I was in a meeting at the marketing agency where I was working, and I shared an idea that would solve both a revenue and communications problem for a client. It spurred a hearty conversation. We discussed operations changes, a rollout process, the branding concept, etc. Folks shared creative builds, cautions, risks, and questions. The room was hot with good ideas.

After thirty minutes, Dean, Mr. Mansplainer-a-licious at the agency, stood up in super-fun khaki dockers and a gingham shirt, removed his fake-cool horn-rimmed glasses with dramatic flair, and in an *I've-got-a-secret* voice, said, "I think I have it." He then proceeded to share—in the mansplainiest way possible—the same idea I had shared forty minutes earlier! I looked up and spontaneously, yet incredulously, stood up and said, "Thanks, Dean! I'm so glad we are going to revisit the idea I shared at the outset. This discussion really helped the idea! You've been a great assistance today. I'll go write it up." It was the nicest possible way to put him in his place, but he got the message loud and clear.

After several years in marketing and advertising, worrying about what people thought of me far too much and hating myself for it, I began to ask myself, *is this it? Is this all there is, persuading people to buy stuff? Is that it?* Since I was very young, I had volunteered at shelters, meal programs, and other social services. After volunteering with dozens of interesting nonprofits, it never seemed like volunteering on the side was enough, and I knew I wanted more: to help people and serve professionally. I needed to reassess, see the signals, and do something meaningful and impactful.

At twenty-six, I knew I needed a reset. I knew deep in my soul that I still wanted to work in some form of marketing or communications, but it could not be in an environment where the sole purpose was to make a company's brand look good and sell more stuff. I needed more. This is the first time I officially hit "reset" with a call to action. It was a pivot, not a build-from-scratch type of thing, but a change, nonetheless. I also knew I needed time to think about it. I needed what I call a "palate cleanser" event to let my subconscious work on the challenge.

The event I needed came from an unexpected source. On a hot evening in early June, we were out at a popular bar in Lincoln Park, where one of my friends from high school was talking on and on about RAGBRAI (the Register's Annual Great Bike Ride Across Iowa) that her mother had just finished. While her mom was certainly not a partier, she was a reliable evaluator of a good time. She regaled us with reasons to sign up for this week of adventure called RAGBRAI. "Huge parties every night. Drinking while riding your bike about ninety miles every day. Cute guys. Sunshine. And the three of you can simply kick back with no worries." A complete and palate-cleansing escape. I was all in.

We packed up our bikes. Worth noting, I decided to buy a mountain bike to ride every day for that week's adventure. It is the equivalent of taking an eighteen-wheeler truck to a street drag race. Further, I thought it was a good idea to *not* train or prepare for this ride at all. Just bloody brilliant. Despite prevailing conventional wisdom here, Iowa is and always has been hilly, just to be clear, and that was problematic given that my bike was heavy and hard to drive up steep inclines. Interestingly, when participating in RAGBRAI, it is recommended to join as a team. My very creative friend dubbed our team of three the "Witches on Wheels" (WOW), complete with pointy witch hats affixed to our helmets, brooms fastened to our bikes, T-shirts with a "WOW" logo, and plastic spiders to be distributed in bars along the way.

Another fallacy I can assure you is incorrect: Iowa is boring. *Not* true. The WOW danced their way across Iowa on bar tops and tables, played softball, won at drinking games, and put curses on rude people. We kissed boys, talked them into letting us draft behind them, and at times held onto their bikes and let them "tow" us. The WOW team giggled, sweated like pigs, won competitions, shared secrets, and flirted with men. We lived our best lives that week. Photos document the carefree, live-in-the moment and don't-think-too-hard-cuz-you-are-on-vacation atmosphere. Deep friendships were established, and old friendships deepened.

I remember distinctly one evening, under a gorgeous midnight-blue sky smack in the middle of Iowa, having an existential interaction with a guy from Oklahoma who was a farmer. He wanted to get out of the family business and pursue a job with his economics degree. It was obvious he felt the government had wronged his family. He told stories, and I told stories. His name was Joel. Joel shared, "Have you ever had to get up at four a.m. and work for three hours—and I mean hard work, moving dirt, herding pigs, wrangling hay bales, moving feed bags—and then get ready for school, go to school for six hours, and then do your homework? And yet, know that you still have four hours of farm work to do?" He went on and asserted, "So you do all of that, and then you eat dinner, help your parents with the house chores, and then go to bed at about eleven—have you ever had a day like that? Well, that was and is my every day."

He continued, "When you see the corn, the pork chops, and the wheat in your stores, remember how it got there." It was the first time I really talked to a farmer from a rural location. He made me think and appreciate their hard work. This suburban girl really started to consider that every time she was in a grocery store. While we both went on to party like fools for the rest of the week, he really made me think about how incredibly spoiled I was. By the seventh day and the five hundredth mile, I was pooped and ready for a real bed, real food, and air-conditioning! Terrifyingly, I look back at those photos and the deep dark tan I sported, and I am shocked it did not result in some form of skin cancer. What was I thinking?

I arrived home, mission accomplished. My mind was fully palate-cleansed! The trip left me feeling spoiled, needing purpose upon reentry to Chicago, and very motivated. Indeed, I proceeded to reach out to every nonprofit I could find, hoping to find a home.

And I did at one of the places I had volunteered with, United Way. I landed the best job ever (which I still believe to this day).

Accepting a position at a large nonprofit filled me with joy, and I felt like I found my peeps. I met a couple of sidekicks: Alice and Mary. We were partners in crime through and through. Our trio was never too far from each other. Working on the same floor, we saw great work, amazing love, and some good old-fashioned misogyny, but we always had each other's backs. Thirty years later, those ladies are still dear friends and exceptional humans.

But it was not all smooth sailing. In my first year in nonprofit work, the fire found me, quite literally: a gun was fired at me and a group of children. Who knew that this would not be the last time my life would be in serious danger?

At the last minute toward the end of a busy day, a group of volunteers headed to one of the UW-funded social service agencies and asked me to join them. It would be my first social service agency visit. It was my second month on the job at United Way. I was smiling from ear to ear watching a group of fourth graders getting ready to rehearse a new dance number in this cozy mini auditorium on a sweet block with mom-and-pop stores on the south side of Chicago.

Inside this community center was an infectious joy. An old-timey, wooden-walled auditorium, it had a 1930s-style tile floor, a small stage, dark blue velvet drapes, and a piano with big 1980s-style speakers that were hooked up to a huge boom box. The music was loud with a heavy beat and really fun. I was watching the cuties do a little breakdancing, and suddenly, out of nowhere, someone screamed, "Get down! Get down!" A car drove by, and gunshots rang out.

I heard glass shattering, and instinctively, my arms pulled a couch over the five kids standing next to me. I wouldn't let anybody move under that couch for ten minutes. They stared back at me with shock, and I told them it would be okay. "I'm sure the police are on their way," I said. Nobody was hurt. I stood up and saw bullet holes in the wall behind the couch. I froze, looking at the kids in horror. Two of them hugged me. I assured them we were fine.

A small sprite of a little girl with sparkly, too-wise-for-her-years eyes, looked up at me. All of maybe seven years old, she reached for my hand and whispered, "I hate when they just bust up stuff for no reason." As if this had happened before. And then I realized . . . it had.

The police took longer than I wanted to get there and did not seem as interested in helping as I'd hoped they would be. When they walked in, they seemed bored and said, "Anybody hurt?"

I responded, "No, just really shaken up." The officer nodded and said, "Can I ask you a few questions?"

Before he could get started, my immediate reaction was "Will these kids be safe here tonight until they go home?"

The officer scraped his jaw and said, "You know, that is kind of the problem; they are safe here and at home, but the in-between is the problem."

The "in-between" worry has never left me. The "in-between" is really about the injustice of underdevelopment in urban neighborhoods, economic inequity, racial inequity, and lack of available childcare. This would be one of many times when the "whisper" of a problem would persist and ultimately become a dream until it became a true-blue, make-it-from-scratch situation. After three years at United Way, I went back to Michigan Avenue and got a well-paid job in upper middle management as a partner at the Chicago office of the second largest ad agency. I loved nonprofit work but missed advertising. The "changeaholic" in me struck again. It was now the mid-nineties, and it was a go-go market with money freely spent on marketing. My new bosses put me in charge of a large auto retailer account. I was thrilled to be back in the mix.

The team was outstanding. Our creative teams were by far the best in the agency. I was still learning how to manage people who reported to me, worked with me, and worked above me. One of my best lessons was experienced from a classic advertising scenario, in a circa 1990s scene. We had just finished a major presentation to the client that was received incredibly well, only to have them serve up a ridiculously large assignment to the creative, research, and media teams. I was the account director, and it was my job to corral all these folks and get them moving in one direction toward a deadline. Not easy. Creative folks work hard but move at the rate of ideas, not deadlines. Media team members are very numbers driven and do not like to think outside of numbers. Research professionals like to have a lot of time deliberating on qualitative and quantitative information. Mixing that in a pot is tumultuous and frequently exhilarating.

At this point in my career, I was just learning how to manage creatives. It was often an exercise in being both a good cop and a bad cop simultaneously. Similarly, client service people rely on the "work-around" to meet deadlines imposed by clients on a regular basis. Guess what? Most ad folks do not like work-arounds. They tend to be perfectionists, and it is against everything they believe in. With these conflicting needs, somehow it always got done. I loved it.

Sometimes it was easier than other times. One of those not-so-easy times was memorable for me. It helped me become a better leader and a better parent. After a long day reviewing creative, research, and media plans, the group creative director brought the final creative concepts for TV into a conference room with the three creative teams. They all presented with great fanfare and then recommended a final TV spot. The spot was great. Funny, product specific, differentiated the client's brand, and memorable. The only problem was that it was similar to another popular spot on TV. I highlighted this to all. They all agreed and started to pursue other concepts, all except the group creative director. He was not having it. He went back to his office and called me back to his expansive office, filled with smoke. His name was Mark. Mark was a wildly creative, generally very amicable, great group director. In fact, his pedigree read like a Who's Who of advertising. At that moment, he was definitely not loving me. I knocked, poked my head in, and saw him on the phone. He motioned me in. I sat quietly and looked out at a gorgeous view of Lake Michigan and Michigan Avenue. Mark kept me waiting for a bit, talking on the phone and chain-smoking like nobody's business. Remember that? Yup. In the nineties, you could smoke in your office to your heart's content—yikes! He hung up the phone and started right in on me. "What the fuck was that, Marie?"

I was startled. "I'm not sure what you mean."

He continued, "You know exactly what I mean. You made Raf and Tory feel like shit, telling them their work was an unintended plagiarism, and now we have to work all night to fix it." Mark went into further detail and ended after a five-minute blustery rant by saying, "Well aren't you going to say something?"

I paused and said, "Thank you for telling me this. It is good feedback." He started ranting again. I stayed silent. He started calming himself and ended with an apology for overreacting.

Ultimately, we were both right. While I pointed out that he had done this exact thing to me in meetings, it was wrong of me to do it, and I felt horrible. I then presented "rules of engagement" around when and how we should be identifying problems to each other and our teams. We would agree to go to each other first, then present issues to the larger group.

While I certainly did screw up, I let my colleague lay it all out, yell, and scream so we could get past it. Admit when you are wrong and let people rant to get it all out of their system. Mark and I became good pals because we both learned the rules of engagement.

By the way, I learned to do the same thing with my kids. Let them scream and yell; then talk rationally (I might scream and yell a little too!). I have said more than once in my career, "Managing ad folks is a great training ground for parents to be." Chef's kiss.

All these early career lessons were disguised in professional situations, but in reality, they created a frame of reference that would be invaluable in all parts of my life; do not fear standing up for yourself or others. This became a mantra, and I still use these tools when I feel uncertain. I also learned that at least one part of my life has to be in service to others, which began a lifelong career of volunteering. Different causes all the time, but always focused on folks who are not being treated fairly.

LESSON: 1. The day at the community center left me with an indelible understanding about what kids go through in their everyday lives. The roots of violence start every day with injustice, racism, and poverty. In a visceral way and with great clarity, I made up my mind right then and there: life was not fair, and I had to be someone who helped change that.

2. Half of learning to manage effectively, in any environment, is making mistakes and admitting you are wrong. The key is taking that learning and enacting course correction.

HOW:
- Carry your anecdotes and learnings wherever you go. These memories will be your guidepost as you navigate new waters. Keep them close.
- Take the time to develop relationships in every workplace. Not every day will be a picnic, and it is much better to have friends around you.
- Watch for signs you may need to change directions.
- This is where my workbook, "A Life Pivot, Made from Scratch" or "Starting a Small Business: Made from Scratch"

might be helpful. Available at marienewmanstudio.com.
- The collective nature of your experiences sometimes point you in a direction you may not have predicted; be open to it. See my life planning guide series on my website.

TAKEAWAYS:
- When you have an opportunity to learn and feel, take it and run with it, but also do something with it.
- That knowledge is a gift from the universe. It is up to you to give it back and build a solution.
- Always admit when you are wrong or need course correction.

CHAPTER SIX

This Night Changed Everything

OUR ELECTION NIGHT tradition was to host our good friends, Marty and Linda, for dinner and cocktails to riff and watch election returns, slice up some deeply held opinions, and absorb editorial comments from various pundits. Usually good fun, particularly when our team wins. Unfortunately, winning was not the outcome on that fateful evening in November 2016.

It was an interesting time in our lives. I had been politically active going back to 2000, but in 2016 I was in hyperdrive, canvassing for state reps, state senators, congressional candidates, and the president. I phone-banked. Knocked on doors. Showed up in parades, etc. So much so that I was ignoring my business. The reality was that I was feeling very restless, burned out, and like I was on the precipice of something new.

That election night, I was feeling powerful as I came home from a full day of canvassing for four different candidates. As a volunteer for Moms Demand Action, a national gun reform activist group, we often canvassed, telephone-banked, and advocated for gun reform at both the state level and congressional offices as part of candidates' campaigns. Going back to 1996, I had canvassed or phone-banked in several presidential elections and helped local candidates with fliers or signs, but for this election, it was intensely personal for me, given Trump's vicious views on the LGBTQ+ community, women's rights, health care, immigrant rights, and gun reform. This time, I was all in helping many members of Congress with gusto every weekend in August, September, and October.

For the twenty years prior, I had worked with fellow gun reform activists and campaigned for Al Gore, Barack Obama, several state legislators, and now Hillary Clinton.

Feeling cautiously optimistic about Hillary's trajectory, Marty and Linda arrived with huge smiles, feeling giddy with the notion that we would elect our first female president.

As our friends sat on the couch, they both marveled, "OMG, another historic election for us!" In 2008, we had all sat in Marty and Linda's basement and watched President Obama win. "Remember when we all bawled like babies, just overwhelmed with sheer joy over Obama? I feel like it will be that kind of night!" my husband sang out while raising a glass in toast-style.

Truth be told, in the two months prior to that fateful day, I was feeling so empowered that I printed out the State of Illinois Candidate's Guide twice and both times dismissed the notion of running in 2018. Looking out my home-office window, feeling bored and disinterested with my consulting work, I daydreamed of running for office. Reflecting on a few of my Moms Demand Action friends and antibullying colleagues asking me about running, I would get excited and then determine, *No that is not a good idea. I'm not the right type. My kids are too young. It's not a good time now. I'm not independently wealthy. I could not do that!*

To be clear, around the time of the general election in 2016, there were a few local Democrats on my last nerve because of their positions on women, and it made me seethe. One in particular was my own congressperson, whom I disagreed with on several topics. Everyone just seemed to accept that he was not pro-choice and not in agreement with most Democrats on other issues. They wrote it off as this: "The Machine will always protect him. He is immovable here." And yet, I would print out that candidate's guide a few more times and promptly throw it away . . . until the time I did *not* throw it away.

Back to election night, which started with a bang with some early wins for Hillary. Then, it got shakier. By 9:30 p.m., the writing was on the wall, and we were all gobsmacked. The room was tense, and I kept trying to point out, "I don't think it's over, really." Jim kept saying, "It doesn't look good, honey," to which I replied, "She has to win. He is evil." It was getting late, and Linda and Marty had to go. They hugged us tightly goodbye, knowing the news would not be good. I was weepy and thanked them for coming. Jim turned to me and said, "Look, there is no question, Trump is awful, just awful, but let's give this new administration a try. I hate his values. I hate him, but as Americans, it is our job to respect the role of the presidency." At 11:30, he said, "I love you, but I gotta go to bed. I'm exhausted. Don't stay up too late."

But I did. In fact, I kept multiple channels on and watched it all, constantly scanning from my computer back to the TV and then my phone. When it was clear on that terrible night that she could not win, and I could cry no more, I finally went to bed around 2 a.m. The next morning, Evie, my newly transitioned daughter, woke up, came downstairs, and said, "I heard. Mom, am I going to be safe?" If she had asked me literally any other question where she indicated fear of anything else, my immediate response would be "Of course, honey. We got this. Don't worry." This time, the best I could muster was "You know Dad and I will work hard to keep you safe no matter what, whatever it takes." I hugged her closely, feeling completely devastated, yet interestingly empowered and energized.

Before going to bed that night, I had saved a Google search on "training for women running for office in Illinois." The first entry was Illinois Women's Institute for Leadership, a.k.a. IWIL. Pulling that search up on my laptop, I noticed it was 8 a.m. already, and I knew I had to be at a meeting in the city at 9:30. I did something I had never done before: I canceled all my meetings, asked permission to move deadlines with several clients, and went back to the saved search. I devoured the IWIL site with gusto. It was a yearlong program with a highly prestigious board of current politicians and politicos/operatives. The process to become a member of the next class of delegates seemed daunting but doable. Given that I only had two days to complete the application and acquire several letters of recommendation, I had to motor.

Staying in my jammies, I sat in my office and rocked out that application. Taking a break mid-afternoon, I fired off a few emails to state legislators I knew through Moms Demand Action and a couple of executive clients, asking them for letters of recommendation. I asked a female legislator for advice and a coffee meeting; she said yes. Check and check.

Uncontrollably, I started having "injustice flashes" from various points of my life as I filled out the application. What was my "why"? Why did I feel the need to go into public service? It seemed as though every question revolved around why I thought the world was unfair or unjust. Well, I did have some issues to grind, and that propelled me.

Childcare and the inequity in our economy were big issues for me, in addition to health care, women's rights, and LGBTQ+ rights. It harkened me back to a time ten-plus years earlier when I was working and had small children, and childcare was the bane of my existence. Employers and our childcare system do not make it easy for parents. I saw a ridiculous level of injustice for most parents and remember feeling extremely frustrated but also a little helpless.

When my kids were both under six, I was at my wits end for childcare. I was on another hunt for a reasonable and safe day care for my sweet pumpkins. I remember an event that was particularly irritating. Calling day care after day care, I landed on one place that was highly lauded and not too far from my house. I decided to call, and the voice on the phone was a little too Snooty Von Snootenstein-ish for me, but I was open to hearing more about this widely loved childcare service just a few suburbs away. I set up an appointment and visited. I pulled up to a spanking new white brick building with white granite pillars. The parking lot was filled with Mercedes, BMWs, and Porsches, and there was literally a mini water park on the side of the building. Hmmm. Ugh.

"Wait, how much did you say your fees were?" I said over the hum of a sleek new air filter system in Snooty Von Snootenstein's office. I do not have a great poker face, and I am sure I showed my disbelief to this admissions director. After quick math, it registered that the fees would mirror a small liberal arts college semester. *Oh, I think I actually said that out loud. Oops.*

Thus began the search for high-quality but affordable childcare. Good luck! We tried an in-home person who was lovely but moved on after two years. Then, a combination of my saint-like sister, Cherie, helping us from time to time, the YMCA childcare group, bringing one of the kids to my office sometimes, and then a drop-off group down the road. Ugh! After a few years of this baby-juggling routine, I was exhausted. I'm not going to lie; I love me some sleep, and I was not getting enough. The funny thing about exhaustion is that it is extremely motivating for me. I knew I had to jerry-rig something.

I was all done with the day care Russian roulette, so I took a day off, kept my babies home with me, and started to research working for myself as a contractor. On this particular day, I remember hearing Quinn playing in his room with his Thomas the Tank Engine train set. "Whoo Whoo, here I come. Hey, get outta my way. I've got a load!" He then erupted into screams of frustration because the individual train cars unlocked unexpectedly, and he had to start over. Welcome to my life, sweetie.

After feeding both kids, I fired up my computer and dug in. Lots of people do this freelancing thing, right? In fact, easily, five good friends I know do it now, and they have been successful. I called them, took notes, researched appropriate fees and the downsides. There were two elephants in the room: 1) I would be forced to do business development and cold-call folks for business (yuck) and 2) selling this idea of leaving a well-paid job to do something on my own to my very practical husband. Funny, number two ended up being a breeze, but I was still wrestling with number one on an icy-cold Chicago day a month later, hustling my kids in and out of friends' houses and my walk-in day-care service. On that day, I was even more exhausted and just decided to pull the trigger. It is never a perfect time.

That was the beginning of Marie Newman & Associates, a business I started from scratch and ran for fifteen years. I needed a job that worked for our family, but it did not exist! My consulting business was very successful and allowed me to see my kids more, afford day care when I needed it, and yes, get some more damn sleep! I guess the "made from scratch" motto started right then and there.

Appropriately, I shared that story in my essay for the application to the IWIL program. By 6 p.m. on that day after the election, I was still editing the application and researching to make it as robust and attractive as possible when Jim came through the door, kissed me, and said, "Are you sick?"

"Nope," I said, not even looking up.

"I thought you had client meetings all day. What happened?" He looked perplexed.

I finally looked up. "The world is on fucking fire. Trump is a lunatic. Some folks need to get out of government and find a new job. I think I need to help them. So yeah, I have not showered, brushed my teeth, or thought about work."

Jim drew in a long breath and ventured in. "Okay, got it. Honey, I'm upset too. I did not mean to judge. I just . . . I mean, I've never seen you in your pajamas at six at night on a Wednesday—ever."

"Well, now you have!" I spat out. Discerning clearly that I was sounding a bit nasty, I gave him a kiss and said more quietly, "I just can't sit by and watch. It's not in me. You know I'm not mad at you, right?" He smiled and nodded. We both knew that was the day I decided to run for something, yet that picture was not to be fully realized until a couple of months later.

Feeling exhilarated, at 6 a.m. the next morning, I submitted my application to IWIL. My newest smoke signal was this: how do I keep my own child safe and women protected in this new and terrifying political reality in 2016? I was about to find out.

Lesson: There is no damn time like the present. Sometimes, when something has been simmering in the background, it suddenly moves to the foreground unexpectedly. The outcome of the 2016 election was deeply impactful to me and changed the direction of my life. I was ready for a change, and I was lucky because I had a very modular and mobile business that I could put on hiatus for a year, as well as a husband who is the sweetest man on the planet. He could see that I was passionate about this, which allowed me to move forward.

HOW:
- There are things that push you into action. Feel them, know them, and give yourself permission to pursue them.
- The best way to know if you are ready to make this pivot or build something is to start with research. In the case of politics, research roles and races you may want to run in or participate as a supporter. Then talk to local politicians and leaders. Get a feel of where you may be needed.
- If you feel the call toward public service, consider taking a look at my "Building a Political Campaign: Made from Scratch" planning guide, available on my website.

TAKEAWAYS:
- Sometimes you have to take a big leap in a new direction. Of course, you have to prepare and research. There are always steps and timing to consider, but do not procrastinate.
- Sometimes your subconscious knows you need to do something before *you* do. Listen to that voice.

PART THREE

Lessons from the Personal Becoming Political

CHAPTER SEVEN

Only a Woman Could Do This

IT WAS NOW January 2017, and we had just had our kickoff session with my new class of IWIL sisters. We all gathered at a suburban convention hotel and started our session work. During the first day at the welcoming reception, I just had an overwhelming feeling of being at home with these women, feeling like we were part of something important. Each sister in the class was a leader or expert in her field, and they were all interested in public service. Even better, they were all insightful, smart, and kind. I felt an immediate camaraderie. I remember sitting at the bar with five of them after our first day, thinking, *Wow, some of us will run for office. Some of us will win. Who will it be?*

Not long after that weekend, I received a prescient phone call. It was distinctive. At this point, I was exploring a run and trying to decide whether I would run for state rep or Congress. My dear friend Steve, whom I had worked with for twenty years, said, "Go big or go home, baby! Do something important that nobody else wants to take on—that's what you do!" He went on, "You are all GSD [get shit done]. This is for you; you got this!" I loved my friend's kind words. I also didn't think I was up to running a federal race, but I couldn't deny the tug.

How did I possibly think I could pivot and go into politics? It sounded ludicrous. Yet it was truly undeniable that I needed to try. I justified it by telling myself, *You have done this before!* Advertising/marketing to nonprofit, nonprofit back to marketing, marketing to management consulting, and then, while running my own consulting firm, helping my oldest child deal with intransigent bullying, writing a book, building a nonprofit, and then helping my youngest child transition from male to female.

"Oh, Jesus H. Christ. I think I can do this. I can pivot," I said to myself.

The notion of the "pivot" in most women's lives is scary, and yet it is somehow truly exhilarating, right? There are all kinds of people who pivot their career or lifestyle. Folks who get restless and move on. People who have lost a job and do something new. Men and women who get divorced and need to earn more money. Some absolutely hate their jobs and learn a new skill. Others are beckoned by a sense of public service, a nonprofit calling, vocation, etc. Truthfully, there was a little of the above for me, but I also wanted to be impactful.

As a middle-aged woman, I did not want to have regrets. I was already feeling like life was rinse, wash, repeat. I worked during the day, made dinner, worked some more, watched the news with my husband, and went to sleep. Important to understand, some of us who pivot just get restless or bored, but some really need a new purpose. That was me. I have learned that this is absolutely okay. A big pivot can be . . . well, *pivotal* to your happiness. To be clear, this was not only a pivot but also would require building a congressional campaign "made from scratch."

My friend, Mansour, told me two years before he died of COVID, "Regrets are much harder to take in your old age than mistakes are. Believe me, take the chance, make the mistake. You will learn from it, or you will be successful. Or both. Don't be afraid." I keep those words close to my heart and live by them. My message to all is to pivot, build something, and make mistakes. Don't have regrets.

I am happy to report that I have made many mistakes, but I do not have regrets. The notion of missing your shot and living with regrets weighed on me. After I actually had time to think about running against an anti-choice, anti-immigration, and anti-health-care politician, I had an epiphany: *This guy doesn't get his district, and I do. I'm a woman small business owner who ran a national nonprofit program and have a social justice bent. Also, I was born and raised here.* "You know what? Why the hell not me?" I posited to myself.

And so, it began.

Giving it my all came easy. In life, when I decide to engage, it is never halfway. I am all in like a mother to a child. I initiated an exploratory run in early February 2017. The goal was to have at least fifty meet-and-greets to see if the district was with me before pulling the trigger on a congressional campaign. Engaging people who were viscerally damaged by the 2016 election and wanted to truly rise up and run with me was easier than I thought. Chatting in living rooms, garages, on porches, and in libraries was how it began. Meet-and-greets across every part of the district were part of my exploratory process and helped inform a real run. It was frightening, fulfilling, and exhilarating.

Running against the "Chicago Machine" and the "venerable" Lipinski family was truly like a Netflix series—no, really, not kidding. Creepy and crazy things happened every day on the campaign trail.

The Chicago Machine was not a game and not to be taken lightly. I knew that.

People would run away from our campaign for fear of being punished by the Machine. After I announced in April that I would run for Congress against the sitting, seven-term incumbent Dan Lipinski, one of the longest-tenured politicians on the southwest side, a colleague of his, who was a state senator, showed up at one of my meet-and-greets and asked the host if he could come in and join the rest of the crowd. She asked if this was okay with me, and I nodded. The state senator was a close ally of my opponent for a very long time, and I knew what he would say. Unfortunately, he pushed the wrong buttons right from the jump. "Ms. Newman, have you thought about starting with the school board and working your way up?" he suggested with a smile. That really made my Irish temper flare. "Senator, would you say that to a man?"

He laughed and assured me, "Of course I would."

"Well, Senator, I have to tell you, I think our school board is doing a great job. I think our state reps and senators are doing a great job. The only one who is not doing a great job is the congressman. He is completely out of alignment with his district. He is anti-women's rights, he is anti-health-care [voted against the ACA], and he is anti-LGBTQ+," I responded with clarity. The senator proceeded to persuade, cajole, and offer other races I "would be better suited for."

I stood up. "You know what I think? I think you know, and the Machine knows that a woman could beat him." He scratched his head incredulously. I shook his hand and thanked him for stopping by. In retrospect, I was a bit harsh with this gentleman who ended up helping me in other ways while I was in office.

The Impostor Monster visited me regularly in the early days of my first campaign. He always comes when I am alone and uncertain. One day, the Impostor Monster was really chatting me up in the car on the way to meet a well-known, older donor who had agreed to sit down with me in the first few months of my 2017 campaign.

Now, prior to politics, I had a long career in business, and I had met with hundreds of executives, and I never felt less-than or even nervous. But politics was a new world, and the I-monster always felt it was important to put me in my place prior to new situations. That said, I pushed that demon out of the car, onto I-294, and never looked back. Having freed myself of that burden, I was intent on having a fruitful meeting. I chose to wear my favorite summer outfit, probably a little too fussy for politics, but I loved the big, bold colors, the sheath style, and chunky bright-green shoes. I topped it off with my good luck charm, my favorite bracelet, from my favorite husband.

We sat outdoors at a café downtown, where folks like to be "seen" having conversations with "key people." A band was playing Motown nearby. I walked up to our lunch, dancing a little bit, with a big smile.

The donor was happy to see me. After niceties and chit-chat, he led with "You understand, of course, that this job is much more than charming people and having a beautiful smile." Well, I remember looking directly back at that gentleman, saying, "I'm well aware of the 'much more' part—because my career has been filled with 'much more.' Let me be clear. You will not find a candidate who works harder or is more willing to learn than me." I grinned and raised an eyebrow. "But let me also be clear about what I already am. I am a very accomplished former founder of a nonprofit, an author, a small business owner, and a marketing executive. Know this: just being charming and smiling is *not* how I roll. I have a strong record, and I stand by that. Smiles are not needed for getting what I want. Smiles are for appreciating and understanding people."

The donor sat there and stared at me. The band played another song. We both took a couple spoonfuls of food. He finally broke the silence, squinted self-importantly, and said, "I know. My contribution will come this week." Wink.

Test passed. For the record, I hate "tests" and "testers." I am always one-hundred-percent transparent, for better or worse, and I always ask straightforward questions, not trap questions. Testers are a waste of time and quite elitist. Don't be a tester.

It was a long, hard, and thrilling fight. There was a long list of silly political tactics that still crack me up. The Chicago Machine was all about intimidation, both covert and overt. One of the first times I was aghast by their nonsense, I was sitting in our Archer Avenue office about seven months before the primary. Our offices were tiny, smelled like marijuana and cat pee, and had ragtag furniture, a bad half-broken bathroom, and virtually no windows, just the one facing the street. After a long afternoon of begging strangers for money on the phone, I was glad to hit the pavement to go canvassing.

My team and I were giggling and then turned onto the side street where all our cars were parked. We all had parking tickets. Huh? I read the sign. We were fine, no rules broken, and yet, I got to my car, and I found a huge scratch on the driver's door. How weird. My campaign team called the police station. "Oh yeah, you are going to have to deal with the city on that. We can't help you," the local officer lackadaisically said. We then asked if he could send a squad to look at my car. An officer arrived and looked at it.

This very kind officer said, "Off the record, ma'am, you are in politics on the southwest side, so . . ." He shrugged, turned, and left.

Canvassing shenanigans started. The Machine's precinct captains would follow our canvases and "sweep" our campaign materials from every house after we completed a route. It was impressive how much time they spent stealing our materials.

It also became crystal clear that I should never canvas alone. Several times, large White dudes from my opponent's camp just stood in the middle of the sidewalk and called me names. Other times, they would hang out by my car and look menacing. Now, please note, I frequently said something derogatory back or (on occasion) flipped them off. I was not a saint and was fed up with their behavior.

Only a month later, our electricity and gas would be turned off at least a few times a week while I was in the office. The first few times, flukes. Then, given the Chicago Machine's ties to ComEd, I knew in my heart that something was fishy. After dozens of calls and threats, I went to the media, and it finally stopped.

Two and a half months before the primary, polls showed that I was within ten points. I also had several key endorsements, including NARAL Pro-choice America, SEIU, Planned Parenthood, several local unions, and a handful of state legislators. Money was starting to pour in. Those organizations worked their backsides off for the next two months. It was incredible to watch the strength of their organizing and fundraising prowess—not to mention their leveraging of relationships with the media. I was finally being taken seriously. I still admire and am so proud of the backbreaking work these unions, progressive groups, and women's groups did for our campaign.

The crowning moment came at our one and only debate. We arrived early. Quite frankly, these types of appearances made me incredibly nervous. Moraine Valley Community College agreed to organize and host the debate, and we were thrilled. Our opponent had finally agreed to debate. That night, I thought we would pull up and see maybe fifty people from the district in attendance. The parking lot was packed. Five hundred people were seated. It was a larger crowd than the recent gubernatorial debate had garnered.

Holy cats!

We went to a quiet room upstairs to practice with consultants and staff. When we came in front of the crowd, folks clapped wildly. It truly felt like we were all running this race together. Another fun Machine tactic was to send hecklers wherever I went. That evening, a group of anti-choice ladies, seated directly in front of the dais, decided it would be cool to chant, "Baby killer," "You are a disgrace to Catholicism," and "Congressman Lipinski is brilliant, and you are a loser" repeatedly, whenever I spoke. Super fun! The debate was lively, complete with outbursts and protests from the crowd. I did a better job than I thought I would, largely because my team and the progressive groups were wonderfully talented and had prepared me well.

The funny part of the evening was that it became obvious from the start that the crowd was overwhelmingly with our campaign. So much so that we were told my opponent asked for an escort out afterward because he felt my supporters were dangerous. So silly.

More endorsements came in late January and early February: Congresswoman Jan Schakowsky, Congressman Luis Gutierrez, Congressman Ro Khanna, and Congresswoman Pramila Jayapal all publicly endorsed me. All progressive leaders. I was on cloud nine. These progressive members of Congress are all amazing public servants (then and now) and took great risk to endorse me. I felt so indebted to them because they took a chance and were brave to buck the party incumbency machine.

Plot twists came in strong doses in this race, but one still makes me smile from ear to ear. A Democratic donor, who had been championing me for several months, called me a day or two after the members of Congress weighed in. She was dear friends with the one and only Gloria Steinem, international feminist, scholar, and cofounder of *Ms. Magazine*. This donor, a lovely woman dedicated to supporting women, decided to take it upon herself to ask Gloria to endorse me. Ms. Steinem came out in a splashy op-ed, several articles, and more. She also flew to Chicago to headline a rally for me and then went back to one of my top and favorite supporter's homes to meet with 200 women. I was walking on air. Gloria was brilliant, filled with hope and joy, and incredibly poignant about losing women's rights. I just remember being in awe of Gloria throughout the day. When she stood to speak, she started with "How is everyone today? Because I'm fan-fucking-tastic, and I am so glad here to support Marie." I melted. This was early 2018, and she was prescient in her next comments: "Ladies, we could lose Roe—and much more." Well, from the mouths of brilliance, that prediction sadly bore out. Losing that election was made much easier because I got to spend a day with her.

One month out, amazingly, we were down by five points. Internally on my campaign, admittedly, I had taken the advice of outside donors and community leaders and made mistakes with my staff. I was less than my best self, to be sure, toward a key staffer, whose only fault was that he was inexperienced and a bit paranoid. I still regret being unkind. I learned a lot about being kinder. During that first campaign, I treated it like a small business, and that was wrong. A campaign is a movement and needs to be managed as such. My shortcomings were obvious and needed to be improved. The last four weeks were a sprint. I will always be grateful to the women's organizations and unions who fought for me and my campaign. They were my peeps, and I would do anything for them.

The opposing camp learned that I was close in the polls and engaged their close allies, AIPAC (American Israel Public Affairs Committee) and No Labels (a political action committee designed to get rid of progressive candidates in primaries) to run hateful and fabricated lies in an independent expenditure direct-mail campaign with TV spots. The oppo machine was in full force. Who knew that would be just a taste test of what would happen to me in 2020 and 2022?

AIPAC and other groups were an omniscient, dark cloud that would follow me into the next two campaigns, which was ironic given that my husband and his family are Jewish, and we both actively worked on stopping antisemitism. I find these organizations anti-American because they are not helping electoral politics at all, they rarely talk about their mission (Israel), they are determined to get all progressives out of Congress, and they are quite vicious, but I will say that they are successful most of the time. It is impressive, in a maniacal way. Hate can be as powerful as love in politics. And to say they hated me was a dramatic understatement. But just wait. That hate got stored up, built stronger, and unleashed in the coming years like a scorned boyfriend who is a little nuts. More on this later.

In the final days of the campaign, I will never forget the student town hall we held at a pizza place. We jammed about 100 juniors and seniors into a midsize room filled with pitchers of soda, pizza, bright smiles, and giggles. We chatted them up and tried to make them as comfortable as possible, so they felt free to be direct and candid. Once we all felt warmed up, I shared stories about me being a mom-dork. I asked about their workload, what subjects they felt would really help them in life, and how they felt about college and culture in high schools.

Toward the end of the event, I decided to lob out an open-ended question with no agenda: *What is something you worry about everyday?* I thought the answers would be bullying, grades, life after high school, weekend parties, irritating teachers, cost of college, etc.

Wrong!

They said, "I think about someone coming into school and

shooting us," "Kids are angry, and I worry one of them will come with a gun one day," "I worry about what I would do if a shooter came in—I think I would freeze," and (this last one literally knocked me off my feet) "My cousin was shot in a mass shooting a few years ago, and I said something mean online last year about the shooter. I'm worried that the shooter will find me." I could not hold back the tears. As a Moms Demand Action volunteer and twenty-year gun reform advocate, I was stunned. As a mother, it was chilling and really shook me.

That night, I asked my kids about it. They said roughly the same things. While we had talked about it lightly before, I did not take the time for my kids to share their deepest feelings. That taught me something new. I need to ask more questions and be more present.

Ultimately, I learned so much, but I lost that race. Losing by 2 percent in 2018 was painful. On election night, it was clear by 8:30 that my opponent had won. I was devastated. I did not concede until the next day. Unexpectedly, dozens of politicians called to thank me for running. I was feeling as though I had let everyone down and wasted their money. I still appreciated those kind words of wisdom offered in those calls.

After the campaign, I immediately began chronicling what to do differently, in a management consultant way. Honestly, when I fail, I always do a full postmortem. It helps me get past it. I truly had no idea if I would run again or not.

My college-age kids both needed me. My husband hated how I was treated during the campaign, and I missed being with my family. I went back and forth so many times about running again. In April 2019, the real reason I decided to run again is that it became clear by then that I could likely raise enough money to win.

One critical lesson in politics is a need for kindness and respect. No surprise or new insight here. However, if my opponents had shown any scintilla of kindness toward me, my family, or my staff, I would have forgiven more readily and completely. Forgiveness and forgetting would be important. Kindness and truth matter, even in politics.

Lesson: Admit when you screw up. I made mistakes in my first race. I was not as kind at times and listened to the wrong people. I had trusted folks who I should not have trusted. Also, I let my frustration out on the staff. That was wrong, and I still feel terribly about those instances.

HOW:
- If you are set on becoming an elected official, more often than not, it takes a couple of tries. Do not become disheartened if you lose the first time. Pick up, dust off, and start again!
- So your memory stays fresh, begin a formal analysis of what you did right, the positive results, the thing you got wrong, and the negative results. A formal postmortem is a really helpful learning experience.
- My political campaign guide will help whether you are a first-timer or a third-timer: "Building a Political Campaign Made from Scratch," available on my website.

TAKEAWAYS:
- Admit, analyze, understand, and put your mistakes in writing so you can improve.
- Whether it is a business, nonprofit, role, position, or candidacy, know what you did wrong in a meaningful way so you can do right the next time.
- Be kind and respectful no matter what. Expect and demand kindness and respect, even from your opponents. Especially from yourself.
- Learning is a lifelong endeavor.

CHAPTER EIGHT

I'm Sorry I'm late, I Saw a Dog.

THERE ARE THREE critical aspects of a successful campaign, and they are nonnegotiable for victory: 1) an outstanding candidate with a strong message and a real "why" burned into their DNA, willing to work their tooshie off and fundraise nonstop like a robot, 2) your opponent must be both bad at their job and unlikeable in some way, and 3) your staff must be a brilliant, resourceful, and highly creative team. The money will come if these three things are firmly in place. By the way, if you don't fundraise enough, you likely won't win no matter what, but there is no chicken-and-egg discussion here. You have to have the three critical criteria fulfilled simultaneously. There are very few exceptions to these rules.

This is why I made certain my team reflected my district. There were brilliant young people everywhere and many interested in my campaign. I got lucky and the whip-smart, innovative, and delightfully wonderful team I surrounded myself with was beyond my dreams. My field director, Pancho, had a magnificent ability to analyze the numbers day-to-day, grab the insights, and make hairpin shifts to ensure we were in all the right geographic and demographic places that would make us most effective, but he was also fantastic with people. My finance team was hardworking and incredibly patient with my frustration around having to spend half the day fundraising. God bless them, really and truly. My campaign manager, Ben, was excellent at keeping the ship afloat financially, driving our strategy, keeping the trains running on time, staying calm, being a great confidant, and pushing hard, all at once. My deputy manager, Nick, a true gem, was an intern from my first campaign and did it all, an absolute renaissance dude to the end. And importantly, he made me laugh every day (and still does). There was truly nothing he could not do well. My political director, Berto, helped me navigate city politics with grace, strategy, and ease. Mara, my right-hand lovebug, was ready and willing to help with anything and grew into a talented staffer in my DC office. She still makes me smile from ear to ear.

Similarly, I chose my cochairs (volunteer campaign leaders) differently than most do. Usually, a chairwoman or chairman on a campaign would be someone incredibly wealthy with bountiful connections. Instead, I chose two wonderfully unique people who really knew the district, the people, and their needs on the ground, but they were not wealthy. Serendipitously, both introductions were chance meetings that may not have happened. I'm so glad they did!

Sidebar: I have found frequently in life that the "chance meetings" and "folks in the background" end up being the most important people in my life's journey. Shadin and Jose were great examples. Watch for those tertiary, "in the background" players in your day-to-day; they will emerge later as wonderful and important parts of your journey.

I met Shadin, my campaign cochair, back in 2017 during the 2018 primary race. We were introduced just after I started campaigning in late spring. We were both at a meeting where we were discussing how Arab and Muslim Americans in my district were being bullied. It was horrible how they were being treated. There were several incidents I needed to understand better, and this group was incredibly helpful. Shadin was a great counselor in that meeting. We happened to sit next to each other, and then we became fast and close friends. Her ability to develop relationships across the district and the political sphere was and remains tremendous. She was invaluable as an adviser on my campaign and later in the district as a leader. When I was in great despair, late at night, she would lift me up and tell me, "The angels are coming," and they did, largely because *she* made those angels work hard.

Jose was my other cochair. I met him on primary Election Day in 2018. Little did I know, he was one of God's helpers who had been walking door-to-door trying to get me elected. We met at a church polling facility. He made me feel at home, hopeful, and he was hoping to run for alderman. After I lost in 2018, we worked together on several campaigns, including his aldermanic race in 2018. We became fast friends; he was an irreplaceable presence, support, and friend in the darkest of days. He galvanized the community for me on the southwest side and made me feel protected at every turn.

These folks brought amazing ideas, a spectacular work ethic, and a sense of team I had not seen anywhere before. All godsends.

I learned a great deal from my first campaign. In my first run in 2018, I knew as a candidate and manager that I'd made some choices and said some things that did not represent me at my best. I learned from those mistakes. My expectations of my team were too high, and I was not tactful enough. I did not raise enough money or have a strong enough field force. Once I was clear on my failings, I dove into the electoral data. It was clear geographically and demographically where I needed to perform better. Now I needed to take those learnings, build a great team, raise a great deal of money, and lean into my backstory even more. A brilliant strategist who started with me in my second campaign told me in the early days, "*Be* who you are. You are a southwest side Irish girl from Beverly, and you need to make that story clear."

Another critical improvement necessary to my win was this: Pet more dogs! And I sure did. I absolutely love dogs. So anywhere I went—but particularly if I saw a dog when I was on my way to an event and already late (I was always late)—I had to stop and say hello to every pup I saw. Dogs are like chicken soup to me. The ongoing joke I shared at the start of every event was "I'm really sorry I'm late. I saw a dog." It always broke the tension in a room.

Finding joy as you campaign is imperative. From the outset, my team and I decided we needed to have my dog, Iggy, a very opinionated beagle, in as many spaces as we could squeeze him into. It was our secret sauce. He was with me almost every day. No matter where I roamed, I met a dog and, of course, fell in love with each one. A recent study clearly found that playing, petting, and being near dogs is calming, brings positive feelings to the fore, and genuinely evokes joy and hope. I couldn't agree more!

As I began my exploration for a second run, there were looming issues nationally and internationally that would bubble up in a prescient way later. In late 2018, several legislative scholars warned me about Roe v. Wade being upended and the rule of law being bestowed on the states. While that worried me a great deal, I started to realize after Gorsuch and Amy Coney Barrett were appointed to the Supreme Court that they were right. Fast-forward to the Dobbs ruling, and that eerily became a truth in 2022. Those counselors were right.

Similarly, I was privileged to have a higher concentration of Palestinian Americans, Muslim Americans, and Arab Americans in my congressional district than any other district in the entire US. The Palestine/Israel issue was complex. My husband is a Jewish American, and we have a huge number of Jewish friends and family. From 2017 to 2019, I worked closely with a series of social justice experts, Palestinian scholars, Israeli scholars, Middle Eastern experts, etc., to better understand this issue.

What was very clear to me, even in the early days of 2017, is that the Palestinian voice and reality on the ground in Palestine were being ignored. The media depicted Palestinian residents as terrorists or terrorist-adjacent. Congress would only listen to AIPAC and far-right, pro-Israeli voices. Over time, I was heavily cautioned by scholars that there would be some form of reckoning and war/other conflict between Hamas and Israel in the coming years. It was a constant drumbeat. While I did believe then and do believe now that the Palestinians have been enslaved and abused, and their land has been a full occupation/Apartheid since 1948, I don't blame Israel. I actually blame the international community who put this action into writing and international law. Both Israel and Palestine have a right to exist and prosper. They should have been given separate, equal, and distinct sovereignty as individual countries and freedom to be self-determined, each with security and a path to prosperity. They both should have been given equal support from the international community. It was not even. That said, we are where we are. In the 2017 to 2019 timeframe, the folks who were consulting me were prescient as well. In fact, they were constantly bringing me new information that confirmed where we landed very recently, a full war and genocide. Interestingly, Israeli citizens did not/do not like their government's abusive behavior and do not support the ongoing horrible treatment of Palestinians. The Israeli citizens are not to be faulted; the right-wing government is the issue.

Given the advice and clear knowledge of the situational reality on the ground in Israel and Palestine, I was so scared that this would turn out the way it actually did (an attack and war). I would continue to keep these advisers close at hand for counsel at all times, mostly because things change frequently and the region is critical to the US but often ignored by legislators. Sadly, I must admit these counselors were exactly right: Hamas (again, not Palestinians but a terrorist organization) attacked Israel on October 7, 2023, in a vile and brutal way. Hamas is evil and wrong, but Netanyahu created a hateful and evocative environment in which this could happen. Neither the Israeli nor the Palestinian citizens wanted Netanyahu to annex land, set up blockades, starve Gaza, militarize the entire area, or steal land. He is a cruel and awful dictator. My heart breaks for both Israelis and Palestinians. To be clear, though the Palestinian voice had been squelched for decades and the brutality of Netanyahu was ignored by Western media until 2022, the Israeli people and Jewish people around the world and in America were not the problem, ever. Netanyahu and others like him in the Israeli government were—and *are*—the problem. I am forever glad I brought in Middle Eastern scholars early and listened to them. They were invaluable.

As anyone who has ever studied history, when any group has full power over another and there is poverty and inequity, wars happen. Brutality happens. People become desperate. I am very happy I listened to my instincts and my sage advisers and continued to press for peace and a two-state solution, ending the occupation permanently and seeking safety and prosperity for both sides. I'm so proud of my Arab American and Jewish American friends for standing up for peace and morality, working to end the occupation and pressing our leaders to lead on this. I knew that this was an ever-changing dynamic that would have worldwide consequences, and there were very few Israel/Palestine advisers available who really understood fully the emerging situation on the ground. In retrospect, I'm so glad I listened and had those precious few folks on my team throughout the 2018 to 2022 timeframe so I would be ready for the inevitable.

Even before I announced I was running for office again, the Illinois Machine tried to scare me (literally), but I had made great friends in huge national progressive movement groups and was encouraged. Secretly, a few party leaders called and sincerely encouraged me to try again. Going against an incumbent? Simply not done, but there was a movement afoot to replace him, and those leaders knew I had the policy background, the desire, and the vision to do it. The times were a-changin'! Some were helpful; others worked against me.

Campaigning is always filled with wacky tricks by various parties to keep you out of the race. One of the other fun tricks about Democratic Party politics is the entertaining antics of the DCCC (Democratic Congressional Campaign Committee), the group that supports all incumbents in their campaigns every two years. Extra fun, they do not care how awful or out of alignment an incumbent is with their district; it is just important to them that the incumbent wins, even if said incumbent is a pain in the neck, is out of alignment with their district on multiple issues, and blocks the DNC agenda frequently.

To that end, they have a technique called blackballing. The DCCC makes it clear to all Democratic pollsters, TV consultants, direct-mail houses, strategy groups, communications/digital consultants, and other campaign support groups that if you support a primary challenger candidate against an incumbent, you will never get any incumbent's campaign business or business from the DCCC ever. Wait for it. . . . yes, you guessed it. That precise problem became my problem, right before I announced.

My original general consultant, pollster, and direct-mail teams said they were "heavily pressured" to bow out of my campaign, right before I announced in mid-April 2019. I had to replace them quickly. I was not angry, but it did make me think, *Wow, the DCCC is really powerful and scares the crap out of everyone*. It also made me think back to my consulting business. I had been pressured in various ways for various reasons to not take clients or—conversely—to take them due to pressure, but I never gave in. I likely could have made much more money, but honestly, I just react horribly when someone wants to control me. It's bullying—plain and simple. By now, you know how I feel about bullying. In any event, these folks all told me about the blackballing the exact day before I announced—super fun!

My exploratory process was a few months long, but obviously I had thought about whether I should run or not. It was a nail-biter. I agonized back and forth from December 2018 to April 2019. My family needed me. There would be huge tension between the Democratic establishment and me. I was transparent with everyone and told them I would not really make a full decision until early April. I never really decided until the day before I announced, on April 15, 2019. It was a huge roller coaster from February to April 2019. Once I decided and was all in, I was clear that we needed to make it fun, well-organized, and strategic, or I simply could not endure the yearlong sprint it would take to win. I surrounded myself with funny, hardworking, creative, and brilliant campaign staffers (every last one was amazing and so very committed).

My staff got to know me quickly. I was a walking suburban mom joke and a dork. It made them giggle. When we knocked on doors, we brought out all the silly every time. I frequently interacted with lawn decor (cement roosters, gargoyles, holiday inflatables, and signs) on social media and, of course, dogs, but my favorite canvassing times were around Halloween, Thanksgiving, and Christmas/Hanukkah. I had full policy discussions with witches, Santa, reindeer, and Tom the Turkey, on lawn after lawn, while canvassing out in public. All caught on video.

One of the most supreme compliments I have received regularly is this: "Nobody works harder than you." Similarly, when folks comment about my kids having a strong work ethic, it just makes me beam. Being smart, kind, compassionate, or attractive is lovely, but those are gifts you are born with, not worked for or accomplished. My whole campaign was about hard work.

We built an amazing coalition of women, progressives, every single community of color, courageous leaders, neighborhood groups, national progressive organizations, civil rights groups, racial equity groups, the LGBTQ+ community, and more. We ran a clean, policy-based-only campaign fight in our ads. No personal attacks. It was mostly joyful, with a close group of supporters who became dear friends.

Here's the truth about congressional campaigns: Lifelong friendships are made . . . and lost. Tragically, the win always feels good after a hard fight, but know that there are grudges, and they come back to haunt you. And, because your values become crystal clear to all who know you, even a few of your oldest friends hold very different values than you. It happened to me, and it was very sad. While I do not regret or feel bad about my values, I miss those I lost due to differences of opinion on immigration and racial equity. That stinging truth became clear after I lost in 2022. Truly, I learned the hard way who deserves trust. And ultimately, I paid the price.

By early April 2019, I had all but sewn up the support of EMILY's List, NARAL Pro-choice America, SEIU, PCCC, and Planned Parenthood. To my surprise—historically, this is never done—those powerhouse Democratic organizations announced their endorsements of our campaign together in early May 2019. It received a great deal of attention. These folks and their supporters had been trying strategically to oust one of the last anti-choice, anti-LGBTQ+, and anti-immigrant Democratic members of Congress (my opponent) for a few cycles; receiving their support was an honor, yet also critical to the win. In 2019, there were only two anti-choice Democratic congresspeople: my opponent, Dan Lipinski, and Henry Cuellar of Texas.

The race was a full-on roller coaster. Sixteen-hour days, every day.

We hired a field team early, and folks started canvassing in May 2019 for a March 2020 primary. We completed nearly 350 meet-and-greets throughout the district by primary week. It was a slow, heavy grind, but momentum was clear by the end of June, and we were getting national attention for being the "little engine that could." *The New York Times*, *The Nation*, *Wall Street Journal*, *Washington Post*, and *Chicago Sun-Times* were buoying our motion forward.

And then, we hit our first speed bump.

Of course, we knew things were going too well. Two other candidates jumped into the race, and *bam*, it just got harder. One of those was well funded. So, it was the four of us, Lipinski, two other men, and me. It was challenging enough to know Lipinski was funded by AIPAC, DCCC, No Labels, and scores of lobbyists. *Ugh*. Early on, we made the principled decision to never take corporate PAC money or lobbyist money. (A PAC is a political action committee, a group supporting a candidate outside of the candidate's campaign.) I was lobbied frequently by several, but I never gave in (a couple times I was admittedly tempted).

We became the letter carriers of politics. Through rain, sleet, snow, dark of night, onto our appointed routes we went. Every day. *No matter what.* The pace was daunting, and when I look back, I somehow feel disbelief at what we accomplished. It did not matter what happened to us; we went to every event, meeting, and festival, no matter the weather, how we felt, or who tried to get in our way. One day, I walked a parade with a 102-degree fever and then did a gun reform forum before going home and making another five hours of fundraising calls.

My dad had a heart attack, and I went down for two days to see him. Please note that when running for office, operating a business, or doing another insane activity, you will never get your parents back after they are gone, so take the damn time to see them! Regret is real.

Upon my return two days later, my nineteen-year-old daughter, who was having a terrible time in her freshman year of college, checked herself into a behavioral hospital after a breakdown with a teacher. Evie sent me a text on a late afternoon in early November. "Mom, I'm checking myself into the hospital." I called her, texted her, called the school. No answer. Called my husband. *Which hospital? Good Lord, where is she?* My husband took over and, but for the grace of God, found the closest hospital to her dormitory and went there. Out of our minds with worry, we hopped in our cars, got there quickly, and raced inside.

Unfortunately, because she was over eighteen, they could not tell us anything. Then we were told she was being sent to another hospital to be put in a lockdown unit. We begged. "Please, she just turned nineteen and is very vulnerable. I am positive she is terrified. Please tell me where you are sending her." Finally, a kindhearted, young intern acquiesced. Evie would arrive at the Berwyn behavioral health center around midnight. She was admitted, her phone taken away, and in a lockdown. More begging. They let us see her for a few minutes at 1 a.m.

For her ten-day stay, my team covered for me for some events, but I still worked the phones, had meet-and-greets, had four hours of call time, knocked on doors, took interviews, begged for endorsements, all the stuff. Then, at 7:30 p.m. each night, I went to see my daughter with my husband. In retrospect, being busy may have helped me avoid completely losing it over her illness. But Lord, I was worried. She came home and seemed to be getting better very slowly. After that incident, my daughter and I would have several difficult times. Her anxiety and depression baffled me. In truth, I did not take time to understand it better. I felt like I had read all the books, we did all the family therapy, so what else? The "what else" was just being there. I did not do enough of this. The campaign became my whole world. I still feel incredibly guilty.

The speed of endorsements quickened. By early autumn, Senator Kirsten Gillibrand, Senator Elizabeth Warren, Congresswoman Alexandria Ocasio-Cortez, Congresswoman Katie Porter, and Congresswoman Jan Schakowsky had all jumped in with their support. I was elated and shocked. Endorsing a challenger against an incumbent is a risky move. These women were brave to do so. I deeply appreciated and still appreciate the risk they took and their kindness.

Being a candidate is a paradox. On the one hand, you are surrounded by people twenty-four seven. One spends every day with staff, constituents, elected officials, union reps, volunteers, supporters, etc. On the other hand, you have a lot of time alone with your thoughts. There was not a single day I did not feel selfish and guilty. Simultaneously, I felt alone and overstimulated. The dissonance was often palpable. And yet, I persisted.

By January 2020, we had momentum: dozens of union endorsements, national women's groups' support, ten members of Congress, and a handful of senators. Money started to pour in.

"Marie, you are five points behind him," my pollster said in a strategy meeting. I was in utter disbelief. It was early February. "This is finally doable," I blurted. The room erupted in laughter. "This is what we have been telling you all along!" I leaped up, did the Molly Shannon superstar pose, and said, "Let's fucking go!"

The next seven weeks would be a blur. Surprise endorsements from local politicians popped up, which was the boost in the neighborhoods we needed. Then the big day. Lori Lightfoot, the mayor of Chicago, endorsed me at a huge event in the storied and famous Beverly neighborhood, where I was born.

The sun was shining, snow was melting, and metaphorically, the ice on the southwest side was giving way to a clear path to winning. We had worked so hard. Meet and-greet after meet-and-greet, community events in every neighborhood, canvassing, phone banking. Finally, the tides were shifting, and many former Lipinski supporters started to convert my way.

On the day of the mayor's endorsement, my amazing deputy campaign manager drove me to the huge event at a famous old church, and we giggled about funny conversations with conservative folks and, of course, cute dogs we had met along the way over the last several months. My best friend, Margie, and her husband lived there and came to support. Margie was always the perfect friend during my campaigns. She would check on me often, giggle about funny political people I would meet, and tell me that she was proud of me. A better friend, you will not find. She made me feel normal in the most unnormal of times. I was so glad to see the joyful crowd of 300 people crammed into the church auditorium. After my speech, Mayor Lightfoot boomed, "It is a new day in IL-03, folks. And Marie Newman is ushering it in!" She grabbed my hand and pulled it up in the air like a prize fighter who just won a fight. The room erupted. Reporters threw out questions, people were kind, and I was so grateful. It was a day.

The following week, a super PAC that had joined forces, made up of women's groups, unions, and progressive organizations, started running positive ads for me and negative ads against my opponent. As a campaign, you cannot ever know about, talk with, or coordinate with a super PAC, but what most folks don't know is that you can send out signals that folks/groups are welcome to help. The signal is a portion on a campaign website called "a red box." Usually short and sweet, with key negative and positive messages, but very clear. When candidates share that they "had no idea and of course did not communicate with a supportive PAC," it is likely true, but they would have known about their site's red box signaling to PACs that help would be appreciated. Don't let candidates get away with saying they "did nothing to attract XYZ or this PAC"—it is simply not true, and they know.

I was getting truly exhausted from asking for money, endorsements, and support. I literally lost brain cells at fundraising call time. Repeatedly asking for money was agonizing!

Then, the world stopped. COVID was all over the news. This virus was terrifying. People were dying, becoming horribly sick. Then we heard about people on respirators.

My campaign manager, Ben, came into my office a week from the primary and said, "So, we have to cancel the election night party. Everyone is. I will take care of everything. We will just have staff, volunteers, and your family here. And yeah, we are going to have to move the door knocking to the phones. Including you, Marie—no more door knocking." I wept because I knew it was the right thing to do, but I thought it might make us lose. I was embarrassed to admit that I was more worried about that than the virus at that moment. By Election Day, it became clear that the virus was lethal and scary. I was glad we pulled the door knocking.

On Election Day of 2020, I woke up and thought, *Well, this has been a tremendous ride. I likely won't win, but I had an experience of a lifetime.* I thought I would lose but was determined to make the best of the day. I masked up and went to polling places, schools, and churches.

Surprisingly, we knew by 9:30 p.m. that I won by four points. A TV announcer said, "Newman, an insurgent, beat sixteen-year incumbent Lipinski." Huge surprise. I jumped up from our smelly, lumpy office couch and into my husband's arms and said, "No way." He said, "Yes way, honey, you did it." I was ebullient. I hugged Margie and my team and collapsed into a chair. Tears of joy and a feeling of doing the impossible washed over me. Congresspeople, senators, and the governor called to congratulate me. I was astonished. It was magical.

Then, COVID hit full force. The state went on lockdown. We knew our district was solidly blue and we would likely win the general election. Yet, we had to keep campaigning after the primary. Nobody understood how to deal with a pandemic. We all learned. Our team worked with the community to bring food and supplies everywhere. We stopped fundraising until the country got its footing. Then, we fundraised again, masked up, and went to outdoor events. By fall, we were back on doors and starting up the TV, digital, and direct-mail campaigns. We won the general election by twelve points, quietly and anticlimactically. We had to coordinate with the party to get ready to "start in Congress." Even the words sounded like a dream!

Freshman orientation for Congress was hybrid, and in-person sessions were with masks. The pandemic made it clear that as a congressperson, I needed to work twenty-four seven on equity. The inequities more dramatically drawn out by COVID were staggering. What was clear before was now like an omnipresent, white-hot light. More horrifying disparities were ahead.

The scariest part was that I would be going into a whole new world with no experience —with Congress or a pandemic. I was over the moon with excitement, but I was also ridiculously anxious. The fires would become more frequent, but I also started a few myself.

LESSON: First, make sure you take time to thank everyone. When you win a fierce and painful battle, make amends with your opponent. I did not do this, and I lived to regret it. While I blamed the pandemic, I could have made much more of an effort to hear my opponent's advice, seek his history of the district, and become friendly. I did not. It was disrespectful and wrong.

HOW:
- When you are in an all-consuming job like politics, entertainment, and executive roles, stay grounded and in touch with your whole life, not just the job. Do a quarterly check-in on your life. I developed the "Life Grades System" that looks at your personal, professional, mental, emotional, financial, passionate, service, family, and values life and helps you monitor if you are living holistically, in a silo, ignoring areas of your life, and more. This system is critical to stay healthy. The chart can be found in my "A Life Pivot, Made from Scratch" planning guide.
- When dealing with stress and family, pay attention to the emotional/mental health issues. The "Family Mental Health Plan Made from Scratch" is a how-to guide for organizing your family while addressing mental health treatments, health-care providers, therapists, day-to-day family supports, etc. Getting a mental health diagnosis is tough, and making sense of everything is challenging. This booklet might help your family organize all the options and take it on as a team. It's available on my website.

TAKEAWAYS:
- Make amends whenever you can. Otherwise, people hold onto resentment forever.
- Resentment is toxic and will hurt you later.
- Pet more dogs! It helps you win.

CHAPTER NINE

You Might Need to Take Your Shoes Off, Ma'am . . .

IT WAS MY third day on the job. As I walked down the sprawling, cavernous tunnels underneath the Capitol, the white brightness of my surroundings felt wavy and Jell-O-like, tinged with my own disbelief at even being there. My mind was racing, thinking about all the work ahead of us. The sharp sound of my own heels clicking against the tile lulled me into a daydream state that was oddly scored with the song "Carolina in My Mind" by James Taylor. Ever since I was a young girl, whenever my mind needed taming or slowing, it naturally would draw me back to a song from early childhood to calm me. The weight of being in that building with the agenda of certifying the election was settling like a twenty-pound hat on my head.

In my daydream state, I was bubbling over with appreciation and love for my husband: the quiet, brilliant, steady force who was always humble, kind, and the most caring force throughout all of what we'd been through on the road to Congress. I felt so much love for my family and friends, love of country, and love for those who sacrificed so much to lift me up and helped elect me to this office.

However, in those early days of my first and only term in Congress, I would also have a daily fight with impostor syndrome.

The Impostor Monster was in full bloom that day, filling my head with questions: *Not sure I should be here? Maybe I should be?*

No, definitely not. Am I out over my skis? Will "they" figure out I do not have what is required to do this job? Dear Lord, help me.

Often, during this fight in my head, I would reconcile, *No, we all worked damn hard, I know my district well, and I fully understand the policies needed. In reality, it doesn't even matter because I'm here! So, guess what? I'm putting in my all and just doing it.*

While wrestling with this Impostor Monster deliberation, I was shocked back into reality with someone waving and shouting, "Congresswoman!" It was midday on January 6, 2021. I was walking alone in the underground tunnel beneath the Capitol. The high ceilings and spacious hallways made it seem more like a vast airplane hangar than a tunnel. These tunnels are used for Congress members and staff to access the Capitol building more directly from their office buildings and other parts of the Capitol Campus. Most days, they are bustling, but in January of 2021, COVID created a time warp, and the tunnels were often vacant. A burly Capitol Police officer approached and said calmly, "Ma'am, we have to go. You might need to take your shoes off. We're gonna have to move quickly." I remember thinking, *Good Lord, I have been running in high heels my whole career. I do not have to take my damn shoes off!* So I said, "I'm fine. Let's just go!" I knew exactly what he meant; he did not share details. His assignment was to get the stragglers out of the Capitol and get them quickly to the safest place possible.

We walked fast/ran seven blocks through the tunnels back to my office, passing other members of Congress doing the same thing, grimacing, heads down, clutching phones and folders, breathing hard. At some point, the officer got called to another location. I remember running as fast as I could, trying not to lose my breath as images of my husband and kids, our dog, my parents, friends, work, my grassroots campaign, that email I forgot to send, the thank-you note still sitting on my desk, the dry cleaning I needed to pick up, and everything and nothing darted through my mind. I was worried about my family, knowing they were probably scared to death, wondering if I was okay.

My mind kept going, my legs kept moving, and I couldn't feel my feet. I just needed to get to safety. When I reached my office, there were a few officers in the hallway who instructed me to get inside, stay there, and remain calm. After I opened the old wooden door, I was greeted by seven fresh-faced, highly competent twenty-somethings (my staffers) looking at me wide-eyed.

My go-to when I'm scared is humor. I slammed the one-hundred-year-old door shut and asked my team without missing a beat, "Do we have *any* wine?" Next, I made sure my team was all accounted for. I gave everybody a job. That day, night, and the next day ahead would be rough, but not as rough as for other members left on the house floor, which I would learn about later. Those members would have a much more difficult time in the coming hours.

Mama skills during times of terror or distress will serve you well. It does not matter whether you have given birth or not; every woman has mothered somebody and has mama skills. I knew that this day would test my leadership skills, but interestingly and almost incongruously, I was at my very best in these high-stress situations and knew exactly what to do. When there is a serious crisis, the number-one job is to keep everyone calm, safe, headed in one direction, and distracted with something that requires them to use critical thinking skills to keep their minds away from fear. In other words, put your full-on Mama pants on and ride that horse to the end.

I had fought a wide array of fires before, but nothing prepares you for being responsible for people's physical and mental safety in close quarters during an eighteen-hour crisis period. And, oh yes, there was the small matter of a full existential crisis for the country. I had been mugged in my twenties, fought for women's rights, was a gun reform activist, championed antibullying legislation, and received death threats in my forties and fifties. Still, a 10,000-person mob hell-bent on a government takeover, well, that would be a new one for me!

January 6, the nation's insurrection. Some say it was the fourth of its kind in our history (other similar insurrections occurred in 1814, 1954, and 1998), but for everyone there, it was the first and only. It is paradoxical, but while enmeshed in a historical event, it is hard to grasp that you are a participant in said historical event. Believe me, it hits you later.

Thinking back to that morning, between my intermittent bouts of impostor syndrome, I was exhilarated, deliriously happy, and filled with immense passion and mission as I walked out of my tiny apartment on New Jersey Avenue, just six blocks from the Capitol, at 8:30 a.m. I was beaming, with my congressional pin on my suit jacket (although hidden because we were told to hide our credentials in public due to the threat of violence). I was ready to crush this day!

It was a brisk forty degrees. We all snickered, thinking these folks outside looked like yahoos, but they *were getting closer*. Huh. Hmmm. *Oh well, I'm not worried*, I thought, and padded down the hallway.

When I returned to my office, my staff's jovial tone had shifted. I opened the door and my chief's voice had dropped; her gaze was direct. "Let's keep an eye on this in your office." She had worked on Capitol Hill for several years, and I had hired her right after I won the general election two months before. I told her, "I mean, they can't get past the police, can they?" At that very moment, we both looked up to see that a group of protesters, now known as the Oath Keepers, were moving military-style in a line, hand on the shoulder of the person in front of them, all camouflage-clad and some scaling the outside of the Capitol building. We were mesmerized. "Shit!" I blurted. The voting bell rang again, and I had to hustle to the floor.

My husband called. "I really don't like how this is going down. I really, really don't."

I assured him, "Honey, this is the safest place on the planet. We are fine. Please don't worry. I gotta scoot. Love you."

My kids had both texted a couple of times, and several friends checked in on me, but by the time I voted and was heading back, I had received another forty texts and calls from various politicians and supporters checking to make sure I was not in harm's way. I thought, *Whoa.*

At this point, I was still thinking, *Wow, people are* really *overreacting.* About every hour, the Speaker's office would send us safety updates, requirements, and instructions. The emphasis became sterner with each contact. I was headed back again when a few senior members of Congress called to check on me. That is when my antenna went up, and I realized, *Hmmm, maybe this is more precarious than I thought.*

I looked down at my official phone and received a text: "MEMBERS: DO NOT LEAVE YOUR OFFICES UNLESS YOU ARE VOTING, NO EXCEPTIONS."

Roger that. Motoring through the tunnels, my thoughts began to wander. *What if they are successful in overturning this thing?* Some news coverage indicated that the crowds, numbering 7,500 and growing, were armed and looking more menacing than at the start of the day.

My congressional desk was easily six-by-three feet and likely weighed 500 pounds. I started imagining my staff and me hiding behind it or using it as a shield as I listened to the persistent coverage on CNN, MSNBC, Local DC, C-SPAN, and FOX.

Pat, my comms director, came into my office. He had been intermittently asking if I wanted to be interviewed by Chicago news anchors. I said no several times, as I did not want to signal alarm or that this was anything other than a simple protest. This time, he suggested, "What do you think about doing an update video? It might reassure folks . . ."

"I don't know. Let's get Nance in here." She heard me and came in. While we tossed that notion around, the voting bell interrupted us, and I was up and out again. As I passed the TV lines, I saw the Mike Pence noose on a TV screen being held by some burly White guys in fake military garb. "Sociopaths," I spit out as I ran to vote.

My mind drifted back to a time when I was volunteering at a gun reform event. Second Amendment enthusiasts created a circle around me and a group of Moms Demand Action volunteers at a rally. They were outfitted with guns and those heavy ammo cross-body belts, Rambo-style. We were genuinely scared because we had diverted from the crowd for a water break. They had spotted us and sought us out. All four looked straight out of a movie perhaps titled *Bad Dudes and Big Guns*, but they definitely weren't actors!

They leaned in, and the sweaty, testosterone-overloaded fireplug leader said, "You smug, anti-American bitches. You hate America, don't you? Admit it. We have every right to bear arms. We won't let you take our rights away. You—"

"Okay, okay, guys, these ladies can be here. Let's breathe and back it up," said a short, bubbly, and pleasantly confident policewoman. They receded. We all relaxed our shoulders and thanked her. I had been protesting for gun reform for twenty years before that and had never felt in danger until that day.

The crowd outside the Capitol on January 6 reminded me of the Second Amendment folks trying to intimidate us that day, but much, much worse.

I entered the house floor with my designated member voting group to place our certification votes. While inserting my voting card, in my peripheral vision, I noted the Capitol Police starting to line every hallway leading to the floor. I decided to get moving a little faster. I voted and made my way past the House floor into the tunnels and then began getting messages on our group Signal chat of freshmen members. Several congresspeople were barricaded in small conference rooms in the basement of the Capitol. This was not a good sign.

What in God's name is going on here? I started to see messages: "I am terrified in this room—they shoved us in here and told us to be quiet," and "They are coming."

Then I saw this on C-SPAN: "Speaker Nancy Pelosi and House Majority Leader are escorted off the floor hurriedly by Capitol Police." This was followed by "Vice President Mike Pence is literally grabbed by Secret Service and pulled away from the podium."

Fast-forward to me back in the office. We had just worked through an exit plan—including who would be responsible for each action should we be attacked in our building—when news got out that the rioters were entering the hallway outside the House floor. Things began happening at light speed from that point on. Phones were blowing up with calls from the district asking if my staff and I were okay. Our team was processing texts, social media messages, emails, and calls. We were receiving multiple messages about barricading in our offices. It was half past two o'clock.

As we turned our attention to the news, it was clear that the protesters had broken into the chamber. I heard Nicole Wallace say, "MSNBC cannot confirm, but we believe that shots have been fired on the House floor." *Jesus H. Christ.*

Nancy ran into my office and shook her head, looking at her chief of staff group text chain on her phone: "Thirty members are caught in the chamber, and it has been breached; there may have been gunfire." My husband called. "Are they protecting you? What the fuck is happening? I don't feel like the House is in control. Are you okay?" I took a deep breath (Mama skills kicking in). "Oh honey, it is not as bad as it seems. Please don't worry. Those MAGA people are nowhere near my office."

"I heard they breached the chamber! This is not just a protest anymore," he interrupted.

I replied, "It's okay. I'm fine. They are getting this under control, truly."

News broke through again: "We have confirmation the protesters have gained access to Speaker Pelosi's offices and are threatening staffers."

CNN was reporting that the combination of Capitol Police and DC Police was not anywhere near enough, and they could not hold the protesters back. While my team and I felt relatively safe in our office in the Longworth building, across the street from the Capitol, while the protest raged on the lawn of the Capitol and inside the rotunda, the mob was strident and not giving up. Turning to my chief, I said quietly, "Honestly, I feel like we are in the middle of an absurd doomsday movie about a bunch of freaks taking over the Capitol, and because we were caught off guard, they win. These people are completely out of their ever-lovin' minds."

Then, a bit of relief. MSNBC declared, "We are hearing that the mob tried entering Longworth and Rayburn congressional office buildings but decided to concentrate on the Capitol itself." I texted Jim. Despite protests, I stepped into the hallway and talked to the police. They assured me, "The rioters are gone from Longworth, ma'am. Please stay in your office." I went back in.

Pat came into my office with an update from his peer group communications staffers' text chain: "Pelosi and leadership are in an undisclosed area safely with Schumer, McConnell, other members, and senators." He looked down with a furrowed brow and read out, "The thirty or so members caught in the chamber have gas masks on and, with the help of the police, are trying to escape." That is when I started getting text updates: "Pramila, Susan Wild, Jason Crow, and many others are among those in the crosshairs," and "Police are guiding them to cover in undisclosed locations."

Information was slow to arrive as it approached 4 p.m., but it began to leak out that someone had convinced Trump to release the National Guard to the Capitol. This was a critical turning point in regaining control. Up until then, the rioters were overrunning the police. Key to note here: only the president can say yes to receiving the National Guard's help, and he has to ask state governors. For the record, all the governors, both Republican and Democratic, had offered their national guards. And they were ready and willing in both Virginia and Maryland to send their forces, but up until then, we were told, Trump would not let them release their guards.

MSNBC, CNN, and local stations shared the same. More phone blowups.

Cabinet members, Chicago Mayor Lori Lightfoot, Cook County President Toni Preckwinkle, union presidents, and others were calling to ensure our safety.

Best friends called and texted, saying, "You probably cannot talk, but please let me know you are okay." I responded to as many as possible, as quickly as I could. Worried district staffers were calling to check and desperately trying not to sound worried.

At around 6 p.m., I gathered the team in my office. I asked, "How are we all doing? Anything I can do for anybody?" Every member was a rock star. They all calmly said they were fine, and we returned to various duties, although none of us could peel our eyes off the TV coverage for long.

Near 7 p.m., we went down to the self-serve market in the basement of Longworth and bought as much junk food as we could hold, brought it back up, and ate chips with little dixie cups of wine.

I remember staring down at my congressional pin, thinking, *Is this a weird dream? Am I really here? Is this really happening?* And then we got word that the Capitol perimeter had been contained and we would be going back to vote possibly by 8:30 p.m. After building two congressional campaigns from absolutely zero, this is where we were. It was all a confusing blur and truly unbelievable.

Calls from leadership came, asking us to confirm that we would be willing to vote once the Capitol building was fully secure. All 435 members said, "Hell to the yes!" And so that very long night began. My chief and I sent everyone home, and as they left, I hugged everyone and said in my mom voice, "Please call or text when you are safe in your apartment." At 9 p.m., we were back placing certification votes. Close to 4:45 a.m., I had completed my last vote and then sat and watched the final group of votes.

At 5 a.m., Nancy drove me home. "Goodnight, Congresswoman," she said. "Oh, Nance," I said, "I think, after that type of day, we are long past calling each other anything but Nance and Marie. Good night. Great work today. So glad you are my chief!"

"Glad we did it all right tonight. See you tomorrow. Please get some rest."

Of course, I could not sleep. Jim checked in and I declared, "Not sure, but I think the police, Nancy Pelosi, and Congress—we all may have just saved democracy today. . . . OMG, that sounds pompous and arrogant." Jim breathed heavily yet quietly. "Hmmm, maybe, but you are very likely right. I love you and . . . so proud of you. I was really scared, honey. I just—"

I responded almost quizzically, "I am not sure I will really process this for a while." I drifted off after I shared, "I love you, pumpkin." Jim assuredly said, "Me too, always." Having a loving partner like Jim was a complete godsend at every turn during the tumult of my two years in Congress. I could not have made it through without his shoulder to cry on and steady hand to make me feel loved and safe.

Truth be told, I did not process January 6 fully for days, maybe months.

When I woke the next day, the text threads and Signal threads were prolific and nonstop.

"I was holed up with three Republicans in a basement-level conference room when we heard the mob running through and screaming for Mike Pence and Nancy Pelosi."

"While I was huddled on the floor with a gas mask/helmet thing on my head, I really thought we would be killed. It was terrifying."

"We held each other's hands on the floor silently and waited. I texted my family goodbye, told everyone I love them and waited. After a long time, the police led us out."

"Thank God for colleagues. My knee surgery left me barely able to move. It took three members to help me up and down stairs."

"They were really going to do it, hang Madam Speaker and Mike Pence. They were not posturing. They were hell-bent. I have never been that scared, never."

"When I heard that shot, I thought we were all going to be dead soon. I cannot even express the fear."

I flipped on MSNBC in my tiny apartment, and it was wall-to-wall coverage. Clarity and deep appreciation flooded over me. My colleagues had been in far, far greater danger than my team and I were that day. Horrific. This was so much more serious than I was able to discern through my bleary-eyed exhaustion the night before.

And that was just the tip of the iceberg. I started seeing colleagues in my apartment building as I left for my office, and it was so solemn, a perceptibly heavy cloud hanging over everywhere. Everyone was grabbing each other's arms, hugging, sharing knowing looks, and the gravity was pulling me into a deep swirl of reflection as I began my walk toward the Capitol. The entire twenty-four hours prior to that day felt like an out-of-body experience that I later reported on to myself—it was surreal.

The next two days, members were inundated with check-ins from mental health professionals, support groups, and offers of every type of assistance from the Speaker's office. Messages from the White House were frequent with updates and stressing, "We are safe, and here are the ways we can help you if you need it."

Taller, stronger walls went up around the entire Capitol Campus perimeter. The police presence stayed at the same level as the day before. As I approached the Capitol Campus, police were everywhere. Instinctively, with tears in my eyes, I began thanking every police officer I passed. They were outside, on the steps, and on the roofs of every building, and after three checkpoints of reexamining my credentials, I stepped inside Longworth. Police were resting on the floors, lining the walls of the corridor to my office. Exhausted, stunned, and quiet, they were ready to help, protect, or just be there as a stabilizing force. I stood for a moment, caught my breath, and offered thank-yous to as many as I could. As I opened the dark, heavy door to my office, my assistant ran around the reception desk and hugged me. Other staffers joined.

I pulled back and said, "Well, that was a different kind of day." Smiling and connecting eyes with each of my team, I offered, "We did it. You were all great. I'm so proud to work with all of you. Now, you are all going to have to forgive me, but I will be checking on you mom-style quite a bit moving forward. I just will. However, we got this. All of you got this. Let's move forward and GSD."

And we did. More horrifying stories came in. Severe beatings, the crushed arms, fingers, and legs the police suffered. The trauma inflicted on the police and the National Guard. Staffers with PTSD. The exhaustion they endured. I still tell the story of seeing police officers holding up fifteen-pound riot shields for hours to keep that mob back. The police are heroes every day, but this group protected our democracy. Later, we would learn of a few policemen's deaths by suicide. I could not imagine how terrified those officers were that day, to have lived through it, but then to be so incredibly traumatized as to die by suicide. The injustice was hard to fathom. I still get teary-eyed when I think about it.

I kept taking breaks to thank God that our country was saved and my staff was safe, at least physically. The trauma would be processed over time and would frequently rear its ugly head across relationships in Congress in the coming months.

Unexpectedly and interestingly, members throughout the caucus checked on me even though they had not met me or knew who I was. I took note. Today, I remain impressed with how our well-being was addressed in the days after Jan 6. It was among the most memorable and heartwarming memories I have of my time in Congress. Speaker Pelosi is a mom at heart, and she used her mama skills during the worst, best, and middle of it. I would see it frequently even when I did not agree with her actions or words. I disagreed with her on several issues; yet still, during that time, she was a leader during the tremendous chaos, as only a tested and true mother could be. It was impressive.

A critical point about January 6 that is often lost in the milieu of reporting is this: In addition to the amazing police officers who kept everyone safe, the Capitol staff were absolute heroes that day. Significantly, I point to the leadership and heroics of Speaker

Pelosi's staff. When that team was under siege, quite literally by the insurrectionists who were charging the Speaker's interior offices and breaking in, they hid under a table in an interior locked office, kept quiet, sent information to leadership to help them and police, all while knowing they could die at any minute. This is but one example of the true patriots we have populating the entire Capitol Campus. These are the public servants who risked their lives that day to serve. Even more importantly, when it is said that the staff run the Capitol, it is absolutely true. The level of resourcefulness, leadership, brilliance, legislative expertise, and single-minded patriotism these staffers exhibit every day is mind-boggling to watch. From the maintenance workers to office staffers, every single one of them makes sacrifices, works ridiculous hours, and is fully dedicated. I marveled at it frequently.

If you get the chance to visit/tour the Capitol, please thank the police, as well as each and every staffer for their work and dedication. They deserve that and much, much more.

Similarly, I also deeply appreciated the members of my state delegation and the leadership team who checked on each of us personally to make certain we were cared for and all right. Further, counseling and mental health care was not just offered but encouraged weekly.

On that infamous day and for the stressful days to come, I keep coming back to and still find that all people are inherently good. Our DNA's foundation was based on a scientific and genetic need to survive. To survive, we must work hard and work together. In these situations where we are being tested, we see the good, the bad, and the ugly. But most people became more exaggerated versions of themselves; a few will lead, most will help, and a few will be selfish.

January 6 revealed that Congress was just like any other group. Most people are good, a few are selfish, and a few are truly awful folks. Let's all keep the good folks in charge.

THE LESSON: We never know when we will be asked to step

up in life. When you are, pull out those mama skills, baby. Let the chaos and tension focus you and give you clarity. You will know what your role is. Your North Star always rises and appears amid chaos. Follow it.

HOW:
- For those who don't know if they are up to leadership, ask yourself the following questions: 1. Has anybody taken the reins and led on this issue? 2. Is the current leader effective, and are the problems getting solved? 3. If you answered "no" and feel passionately about the problem, it is likely time for you to lead.
- In the moment of crisis, your North Star will emerge, and all will be clear; trust this.
- I don't have a planning guide for this type of life fire, but listen to your instinct and your better angels.

TAKEAWAYS:
- When asked to support and follow for the greater good, do it.
- When asked to lead a small group, do it.
- When life presents tough problems, lead with resilience.

CHAPTER TEN

How the Hell Did I Get Here?

A FTER RUNNING AT full speed with my backpack and roller bag in tow through the DC airport, I arrived at the gate just in time and plopped into my seat—always exit row number seven on the aisle—when it hit me: I *just* lived through something much bigger than all of us, as a very small player in a very large and historic turning point in our country's history. An attempted insurrection. It was beyond my ability to comprehend fully. I still had not processed it. Yes, it actually happened, and I was there. *Brain, please help me absorb and translate.*

Clearly, my mind was still exhausted, but I was starting to process things as I sat in my seat. I chastised myself: *Why did I not take notes? Why did I not document anything with words or photos? Huh.* Too much stimulation at the time? Too much to take in? Looking back now, I feel like I was in some level of "fight-or-flight" mode for twenty-four hours.

My plan was to use the hour-and-a-half flight to sleep. That did not happen. A woman two aisles back recognized me, walked up, and tapped me on the shoulder as we were waiting to take off. "Congresswoman?" A woman in her thirties, wearing a trench coat, her smile timid and her large, sympathetic eyes deep with concern, asked, "Hi . . . sorry . . . I live in your district. Are you okay? Oh, my God. That was so scary. Are you okay?"

Instinctively, my mouth formed the words before I could think. "I'm well. Thank you for the kind words. I'm fine, really," I assured her.

"Can you share anything? How did it come to this?" she pleaded.

Without a thought, on automatic pilot, I responded, "We are in excellent hands. The White House and our leadership team in the House are working day and night to assure safety and security at all times. We will all get through this. I know it sounds cliché, but we will be stronger, not right away, but truly, we will be stronger and better." I gathered her hands in mine and said, "You know, God has the best sense of humor; he likes to send two punch lines at once to keep us on our toes, a pandemic *and* an insurrection. Boom and boom. I think He has a lot to say to us, and this was His way. So, let's hear it and all work together." We shared anecdotes about when the universe or God had made us listen. Then the flight attendants said, "Please return to your seats."

She walked away, smiling with a nod, thanked me, and sat down with a disconcerted look. She had gotten me thinking. *How did we get to this point? How did I get to this point? Why was I a part of this?* I thought back to when I was in the tunnel in the Capitol before we had to go on lockdown—just three days prior. *Was it really only three days ago?* It seemed like a month. The impostor syndrome debate in my head seemed silly now. Self-absorbed, really. I reconciled, I may not always feel fully capable, not always ready for what was in front of me, but I'm here to tell you, I got her done, baby. And I reasoned (I think I always have), I need to buck up for what's ahead.

Focusing on the leap from doubting myself to "gettin' her done" was not new territory for me. As my late aunt said so often and directly, "The only way you are going to get it done is to do it. I hate to tell ya . . . there are no shortcuts." This was no different.

When we take a minute to reflect on our lives, I think we forget that dreams sometimes come in a whisper or soft comment; they don't come out raging like a bull. There is no thunder-and-lightning event at first; it usually comes quietly. Listen to the whisper. If the whisper is persistent and the problem associated with the whisper continues, listen. After years of working on issues such as gun reform, bullying, women's rights, LGBTQ+ rights, economic inequities, health-care inequity, and more, the cumulative effect is that the whisper helps us dream and realize "Nobody is coming to save us; *we* are going to save us." In that frame, building something from scratch has always started with a whisper of injustice that necessitates building a solution from scratch for me.

I have built things from scratch at every turn in my life, and this was no different. Nobody knew how to do COVID. We all figured it out together. The folks I built my first campaign with were all smart and willing, but we did not really know how to do it.

The next two years would be no different. We would figure it out.

Always important, when building something from scratch, is to find bakers and builders all around to help solve problems and increase your quality of life so you can be empowered to follow your dream. My husband was and is an amazing parent and husband, incredibly talented and kind. But had he not been working hard in his own career with a wonderful job, there is no practical way on Earth I could have built anything. Similarly, my friends and family were the greatest cheerleaders, who nudged, loved, encouraged, and supported me.

If not for all that support and love, nothing in my life would have been accomplished.

As an example, conventional wisdom for women in politics has been the following: "Women have to work ridiculously hard and then have to be *asked* to run," followed always by "then we have to think about it for a very long time, sweat it out, and then determine we can't." Inherently, women do not like to impose on people and ask for help. On the other hand, men usually just wake up one day and look in the mirror and say, "Yeah, my hair looks good. I could do this. I could run for office and win. I think I will."

This is why only 29 percent of Congress is made up of women, when it should be 50 percent to be truly representative of the country. It is improving, but please know, women make it better by just getting it done and asking for help to build and solve. Women builders, please know that people want to help you because they love you, but remember, they are helping with the building of the solution—such as political engagement, running for office, etc.—because it is fulfilling.

Women tend to think they are never enough. Never fully qualified. We don't have <u>all</u> the credentials. Not quite the set of experiences or the right expertise. However, most men think they are enough. Well, an important note here: You are enough. Period. Full stop. And you deserve to keep growing, keep learning, moving your life forward, and doing it the way you see fit. When Impostor Monster rears its head, reflect and own your "enough-ness." You are enough.

As I sat on the plane that day post-January 6, reflecting on the events of the week, our country's divide, our less-than-functional House, the pandemic, my family, and my career, I came back to this: *How did I end up in this role?* A member of Congress, a leader, responsible for and to hundreds of thousands of voices, making tough decisions, critical changes, and hopefully getting it . . . mostly right? I could not help but think of the various fires I've walked through to get where I am today. The fire I just went through was clearly the most challenging of all, but fire is always present in my life, so maybe my life experience was the reason I was here. The fires I found and the fires that found me.

Those fires included an abortion at nineteen, mugged at twenty-five, and sexually molested at twenty-six. Of course, in my thirties, there were the typical standard discriminations most women undergo at work, and those were just a sampling. Fighting to stop the bullying of my child, writing a book, creating a national nonprofit to help end bullying, and advocating for gun safety laws for twenty years—all were filled with fires. Helping my child transition from male to female in my forties? A big one. Protecting her from discrimination, then and now, is a constant fire. Getting so angry about all the injustices that I set aside my family and career to run for Congress in my early fifties. Then actually winning mid-fifties. I guess my circuitous route was not typical. But is the building of any solution in life typical?

Okay, when you put it that way, maybe it does make some sense how I got here? I am enough. Still, I had never as much as run for student council in high school. What made me think a successful business career and nonprofit experience made me "enough"? Most people run for county or state positions first. For me, all the folks in those positions at the time were doing a great job, and I did not want to displace them. Why fix something that was not broken? But I did see problems and other broken areas in a few elected officials and felt, *Why not me?*

So, what exactly was it in each of those fires I walked through that, collectively, made me feel like I could take on the audacious move of running for Congress?

With each fire, there was no manual, no standard solution, no one perfect way. Often, I had to lead the way without much counsel or help, mostly because it wasn't available. I am a dog with a bone when it comes to problem-solving, particularly a problem involving injustice.

When you don't see the solutions you need or want in the world, sometimes you just have to make it from scratch. So, I did and ran for Congress. There were many reflections and life learnings I chewed on during that flight.

As I wrote in my Substack column in October 2024, I reflected on friendships as well:

After a good deal of reflection as the flight progressed, I finally began to appreciate my family's terror on that awful day. All the incredibly kind close friends, relatives, neighbors, and colleagues who reached out during that twenty-four-hour period to check on me flooded back. Between calls, texts, DMs, and emails, I received hundreds of inquiries and well wishes that day. It finally hit me, and

I began to cry. I hadn't really absorbed the events of that day yet. I looked back through some of the kindest messages. Among them were immediate and extended family, dearest friends, acquaintances, and congressional leaders who did not really know me but wanted to make sure I was safe.

It finally crossed my mind: a couple long-term friends, who I had drifted from a bit, had not reached out. I was surprised but suppressed judging it because I assumed they were busy.

Thinking further, it began to nag me like an unreachable itch in your inner ear. If roles were reversed, I would have certainly reached out via text or to their families. I asked my husband and kids if they had received anything. They had not. Hmmm. After busying myself with some necessary reading and a quick nap on the plane, we landed. I decided to let it go.

A few days later, as I sat in my office, an old friend from high school stopped by to say hello and "welcome me to the neighborhood" with donuts. We had not seen each other in over fifteen years. We chatted for a long time, and at the end of the conversation, he asked, "Hey, how are your pals Tara and Jenny [not their real names]. I am sure they were beside themselves on Jan 6." I offered a generic answer, and we wished each other well.

There it was again. I gave it some thought on the snowy, rush-hour drive home and had to really face what that meant. Okay, they did not call or text, but was it an intentional snub? Certainly, since I entered politics, we had drifted a bit. Further, their views on immigration, racial equity, and health care differed dramatically from mine, but weren't we still close friends? Our families had spent holidays together. We were very close at one point. Finally, I had to ask myself, *When was the last time we spoke, and were we still close friends?*

My answer saddened me. Truthfully, not sure. Did we stop being friends? Did their support of Trump and MAGA offend me so much that we went from drifting to not being friends?

After trudging through the fresh snow, I walked in the kitchen to my husband, waiting with a huge hug and a glass of wine. We talked about this notion of losing friendships over Trump. My husband was angry they had not checked on me, but I felt differently. *Did I deserve to not hear from them?* After all, I had not kept in close contact and felt that I just could not listen to some of their views anymore. *Was it possible they did not understand how frightening January 6 was for the whole country? Was I the judgmental one?* I began to mourn the loss of friendship because it was much more real after my introspection. I shed some reality-just-slapped-me-in-the-face tears.

As the weeks went by, I saw posts from conservative friends on social media depicting January 6 as a simple protest being "overblown by the libs." Then a very memorable day came. The two close friends who had not reached out had been posting about the importance of "stopping the steal" and the righteous nature of the patriots on Jan 6 who tried to "keep President Trump in his rightful position." I was devastated.

At that moment, I really understood how divided we were as a nation. If that event could dilute or divide forty-year friendships, then clearly this was happening elsewhere.

Over the next month, I opened up about this fissure in friendship, and I learned that many people in my orbit were feeling the same way here in the Midwest and across the nation.

I could have probably done a lot more to at least keep the lines of communication open (other than birthday and holiday wishes) and try to assuage my conservative friends "fear" when it came to progressives or liberals. And I had to admit, at best, those relationships were highly diluted. At worst, they were broken. Or somewhere in between.

I have berated myself for not trying to "talk it out" with them. I know I won't change their minds, and they won't change mine. So here I stay, in the murky middle. I have great memories of simpler times and think well of them.

I like to put these matters in the "time is your friend" column and wait it out. I hope I see a sign at some point. Until then, I commiserate with others in similar situations. There may be no answer, but there is the potential for great learning.

LESSON: Life is a little like an impressionist painting. When you are right on top of it, you cannot tell it is a beautiful landscape of flowers, but when you take several steps back and look, they are lovely, have clear definition, and make sense.

HOW:
- Be sure you have these life reconciliation discussions with yourself occasionally. Just like the "Life Grades Chart," think about "how you arrived" where you are and make sure you want or need to be there. This chart is available in all of my planning guides on my website.
- My "Life Made from Scratch" series offers planning guides to organize and address life fires.

TAKEAWAYS:
- When something looks fuzzy or you notice a problem, listen; let it marinate.
- You may be the problem solver. You just may not know it yet, but if you take a step back to look clearly at it, you realize you do see the solution.
- Listen to the whisper and remain open to the possibilities.
- Let your life's experiences shape the solutions of the future.

CHAPTER ELEVEN

Insurrection—My Introduction to Congress.

IT WAS DEFINITELY not on my bingo card to have both an insurrection and an impeachment occur in my first two weeks on the job. Good Lord!

The day we were sworn in as a group of freshman congresspeople, the wonderfully kind staff at the Capitol and from all around the US House campus kept telling us how sorry they felt for us during orientation because COVID restrictions prevented the time-honored traditions of a typical orientation: "You are missing out on the extravagant dinners, the special meetings with the president and his cabinet, and X party or Y event." Truth be told, I did not mind. I was so incredibly thrilled and honored to be there, I did not need the super fancy parties of a normal congressional kickoff. My team and I worked hard to get there; I was just glad to have arrived.

Hand to God, on day three, January 6, 2021, I had just learned how to get to the Capitol from my office without getting lost and where the ladies' room was near the House floor, when, quite literally, *boom*! We had an insurrection on our newbie hands!

Next up, we had an impeachment inquiry. I remember a lot of Republicans who could not even look up to meet others' gazes in the hallways; it was a troubling time. They were hardened and fraught with defensiveness. A Southern Republican lawmaker, whom I liked and had chatted with in the halls or elevators, said, "Can I say you look beautiful in that pink suit today? I know I'm not supposed to, but you are one of the nice ones. I don't agree with some of your crazy ideas, but you are respectful." I thanked him and asked, "What do you think about Trump's impeachment, really?" Well, that set him off. "He is innocent; it was a rally—they were tourists. This is gaslighting." Okey dokey. I backed up and wished him well. Lesson learned. Funnily enough, the compliment about my suit was genuine, and I appreciated it.

Who knew that my term from 2020 to 2022 would be historical, that I would become controversial, and our team would learn how to put out fires with one arm tied behind our backs, blindfolded and without a net, every week? But things were just getting started!

The early days of my term felt like a dream (or as dreamy as it could be during COVID times). My congressional office team was a robust set of rockstar staffers, and we were in lockstep: we worked hard, had fun, and remembered that constituents were the reason we did this job. Our mantra was the following: "Leadership is about empathy and flawless implementation." Boring yes, but absolutely accurate with our team.

We started cranking out legislation, innovative in-district programs, and new pathways that engaged the community. COVID was raging. My staff and I hunted down hand sanitizer, milk, bread, potatoes, and diapers for constituents and families. Literally every day. There was so much agony all around. I was so proud of the amazing nonprofit network in my district. Absolute heroes, every single one of them. Collaboration and kindness were a constant thread across clinics, faith groups, community nonprofits, grocery stores, businesses, neighborhood groups, and residents. I still look back on those very dark days and am nothing but inspired.

On a very cold day in 2020, I was driving to a community event in the city. My team and I got a call from two nuns from the Sisters of

Mercy. They were delivering blankets, food, and supplies to a shelter while protesting the horrifying treatment of immigrants. They were having trouble getting folks to rally because of COVID. We turned the car around and headed their way.

We pulled up, and two sisters in their eighties, bundled up with protest signs and passion shining through their masks, stood there. All by themselves. A few others showed up with more supplies. Immigrants were being ignored during COVID. So, we stood out there with signs and took turns delivering items. I could not stay, but the others hustled supplies, worked with community groups day and night, and protested during the day.

To this day, those sisters, Pat and Joann, are huge influences and role models for me. They regularly fight for immigrants, workers, and marginalized communities, with little support, and make the establishment angry. (They did a super-cute video endorsing me during my campaign and got in serious trouble with their national Catholic order of nuns. When I called to thank them and ask how "the trouble with their bosses" was going, they twinkled and said, "We told them it is never wrong to do the right thing.") I love them so much. I will never forget their persistence and deep compassion. I still text them and ask for their prayers when I need a boost.

I was the first woman to represent the district—proudly—and we were setting historical program service records. My legislative team was spectacular at making the case to address a problem and find its solution. Similarly, my office was designated "the third most prolific lawmaker" by *Axios* in that group of freshmen lawmakers. They highlighted our exceptional team, great work, and amazing support. It was a dream—until it wasn't.

But first, some love. Forever in my heart will be the congressional members who gave me great advice, supported my committee placements, or offered me a robust welcome to the chamber. Contrary to popular opinion, there are great minds, authentic souls, and dedicated public servants in DC.

About one month in, I attended a progressive caucus meeting, where I pressed hard on bringing back the Medicare for All bill to the floor. I was seated next to the amazing Congresswoman Barbara Lee (who recently ran as the only progressive in the highly competitive 2024 California Senate primary to replace Senator Feinstein). Barbara's robust and genuinely warm laugh was welcoming and filled with wisdom, authenticity, and grace. She made me feel heard, while providing wonderful counsel on equity provisions that could be added to the bill. When I turned to thank her, she wisely and warmly stated, "Nobody shared this stuff with me when I got here; I am glad to help." And she did, always. She was and is a lovely human.

Another lovely member was Don Beyer from Virginia. Filled with institutional knowledge, he had similar family challenges and worked really hard. He was a senior member with lots of accomplishments, but you would never know it. Always kind, extremely generous in every way, and welcoming. Each cycle, he would call new members before they started to let them know he was there and ready to answer questions. He was not the only one who did this, but he was one of the few who actually lived up to it. He chaired the Joint Economic Committee and was incredibly humble about the amazing work he and his team produced.

But the negativity began about two months into my term. God always has a ridiculous sense of humor with me, truly. Out of 435 possible office neighbors in the US House of Representatives, God placed me across the hall from the notorious Marjorie Taylor Greene.

Right out of the gate, she determined it was a good idea to try to block the Equality Act, which protects the rights of the LGBTQ+ community, and she called me a "groomer" (she found out my daughter is a trans woman). What she did not understand is that it's never a great idea to bully a former antibullying expert. Ultimately, we helped her to understand this using visual aids and easy-to-understand language, so as to not confuse her about the LGBTQ+ community.

In February 2021, we would vote on the Equality Act. I was

ebullient. The day before, I had given a speech on the House floor about the importance of ensuring all LGBTQ+ folks had rights. Toward the end, I caught myself off guard and wept at the thought of my daughter's struggle to be her authentic self. My thoughts were drawn to homeless trans kids who had been rejected and unloved. Despite our family's constant support, Evie would have challenges in the workplace and with housing, finances, and the public (in some areas of the US and abroad).

Despite these challenges, when Greene started name-calling, I smiled from ear to ear. My creative and wonderful communications director, Pat, could feel my enthusiasm and wanted me to do a video. We shot a video of me installing my trans pride flag in the flag holder outside my office, directly across from Congresswoman Marjorie Taylor Greene's office. At the end of the video, I swished my hands together as if to indicate "all done," signifying I had completed the task. We thought it was just a quick tribute to the Equality Act.

Nope. It went viral. Because Greene is dangerously anti-LGBTQ+, she and her supporters took it as a direct challenge and went absolutely bonkers! In turn, Team Greene literally went to a local printer and produced a bigoted and gross sign, reading, *"There are two genders: male and female. Follow the science."* She plastered it on the wall next to her office.

The whole series of actions went viral and resulted in nonstop media coverage for weeks. I was amazed at how the media thought the fight between a MAGA Republican and a progressive was the most important part of the story, not that she was a bigot and our country needs to come to terms with all forms of bigotry, hate, and discrimination.

That evening as I walked home, feeling the weight of chaos, I came upon Congresswoman Katherine Clark, the assistant speaker, on the sidewalk. "Marie, Marie!" she exclaimed. "Dear God, that woman is hateful. I want you to know we are behind you. Please know we are with you." I could not have needed to hear that more. She invited me and several other congresswomen over for dinner the next night. I was so grateful to not be alone.

A few Republicans found me on the House floor and said they were sorry for Marjorie Taylor Greene's behavior. This is not typically done. I was appreciative and kept their confidence because they did not wish to be public about their embarrassment. It did not mean they supported the Equality Act; they simply did not agree with her hate and felt badly for me.

During this kerfuffle, there were two Republicans whom I still think of as some of the most decent and kind people I encountered there. On day three of this ridiculous feud story arc between me and Marj, I went into the ladies' room off the House floor, and Congresswoman Liz Cheney was coming out. I looked up and, never having met her, simply smiled. She stopped, touched my arm, and warmly offered, "I hope your family is okay." This restored my faith in women who do not share my perspective, who can be nonetheless thoughtful, kind, and decent.

Cheney and I do not share many values, although probably more than I think given her patriotic support of Democrats in 2024, but I appreciated her kindness, no matter what. Further, she is one of the reasons we have a democracy/republic still in place because she did the right thing and voted to impeach Donald Trump. We are a blended government model; we have attributes of a democracy and a republic. Liz is a real one and understands this. I always thought of her unusual kindness and empathized from afar when her party treated her so despicably.

Another real one was Congressman Adam Kinzinger, a Republican from my state, Illinois, the one and only person from across the aisle who publicly registered his dismay and disgust on Twitter regarding Greene's bigoted behavior. I called him, and we had a short but lovely conversation. "Adam, I just want you to know that your kindness meant a great deal to me. You are lovely to support and defend me, but more importantly, to call out hate."

"Marie," he started, "I know we do not share the same perspectives on a few things, but what she did was just beyond. I'm so sorry. Please know we [Republicans] are not all like that. We can disagree and be respectful." I thanked him. It made me optimistic for the coming months and resurrected hope that both parties could work together.

The incident with MTG brought to light another observation: the quizzical "jump on the wagon that is getting the most attention" syndrome in DC. Many of the Dem members who made public statements to support my family are lovely, sincere, and well-intended, but some, let's just say, are more interested in attaching themselves to negative things that will give them a positive lift and publicity if they support it. My team and I secretly giggled at the members of the House and Senate who made loud, televised statements in support of the LGBTQ+ community and my family after they saw the truly ludicrous amount of attention the video received. These same folks—who leveraged an opportunity to attach themselves to a situation that was not theirs—literally could not pick me out in a crowd, then or now. It's still funny to me.

After the second day of this ridiculous arc, I refused all requests to major media. My point was to share that the trans community has rights and should be respected and embraced. Simply acknowledging and "tolerating" was no longer enough. I was not interested in a cat fight; I wanted my daughter and her community to feel safe and stop fearing the world. It finally died down a week later because I refused to give the fire oxygen.

Finally, it must be said, opinions are not welcome in Congress unless they happen to be the opinion of the majority in one's own party. A prime example? Universal health care. During my time in Congress, nearly 70 percent of Americans believed in a single-payer health-care model. My model was a hybrid that I still think would be wildly successful today: using Medicare as the overall apparatus to administer health care and then having the current insurance companies act as vendors for claims and databases.

New Dems (centrists) and Blue Dogs (conservatives) in the Dem caucus mostly refused to listen because very few had strong business backgrounds or health-care expertise and could not or would not understand. Other centrists and conserve-o-Dems just did not want to make the insurance companies angry because they received millions of dollars in corporate PAC money to their campaigns from these health-care corporations. Pramila Jayapal and Bernie Sanders were the brainchildren of the current Medicare for All bills at the time and were magnificent at the technical level and implementation. While I was a huge fan, I would have loved to have had the time to address and make the bill even more practical. They had worked hard for years to be heard, so I understood why my newbie voice did not matter much, particularly when I slammed health insurance companies regularly. The same was true about my opinions on advancing workers' rights, including requiring every board to have a labor member. And small businesses should not have to pay the same taxes as the Fortune 500. On and on, nobody wants to hear your opinion unless it validates the majority. Roger that. Got that message loud and clear in week four. Unfortunate but true.

LESSON: The media wanted the "fight" between MTG and me to go on and on. I ended it by making it clear that I told her how I felt, and now I was moving on. Ms. Greene never really stopped harping on it, but my team and I simply ignored her. She would try to resurrect it from time to time, and we would mostly just laugh and walk away. It's crazy, but she is still talking about it at this writing. Everybody stopped listening to her, and it just makes me laugh.

HOW:
- Let your instincts guide you, and use the golden rule. Do not let an unnecessary or unkind fight keep going.
- Understand the greater good. Don't seek immediate gratification through anger or spite. Follow your North Star

and stay on your own track; don't jump tracks.

Takeaways:
- Don't ever let people bully or railroad you.
- Don't pour fuel on the fire.
- While bullying is particularly bad in politics, it happens everywhere.
- When you see bullying, call it out.
- Always take the higher ground, but don't get walked on, ever. Let the bully know they are absolutely wrong, and then ask them if you can collaborate and be partners instead of working against each other. Even if the bully refuses to partner, you have signaled that you are moving on and your expectation is that they will too.

CHAPTER TWELVE

There is Never Any Time

THE PACE WAS truly daunting. I frequently worked seventeen-hour days, especially when I was in DC. My father, who had been sick for months, passed away just three months into my term. To this day, his passing will wash over me like a tank because I did not take the time to fully grieve.

There were lots of highs and a couple of lows the first year, but mostly I had observations. Lots of them. When you become overly focused, you learn a lot about yourself, but sadly, you let everything else fall away: relationships, feelings, compassion, empathy, and open-mindedness.

Walking to and from my Barbie-doll-size apartment in DC was always an exercise in philosophy. Every time I walked to and from, there seemed to be a heavy weight to strap on and think about. On a wildly humid morning, carrying my suit jacket in the sticky crook of my arm as I hustled up to the Capitol, I knew I was being "DC Marie." I hate her. I had easily spent three hours on the phone fundraising the night before and had forgotten once again to return a call from my closest friend. She was calling to tell me her husband had cancer. My failure to call her back was simply not acceptable, and I will never forgive myself for it.

When I did talk to her in the morning, I felt like a rock hit me. I was so busy begging for money, I could not stop to take a call from my BFF. It was one of those conversations you have more frequently in your fifties. Her husband, whom my husband and I adore, had colon cancer. *Goddamn it. Why is it always the lovely people who get sick? No really, why?*

My heart hurt for them. I admonished myself and admitted that I had become completely focused on fundraising. *Gross, just gross.* I felt transactional. No, I *was* transactional. Not just about fundraising. But, in three months, I felt like everything in Congress was a transaction. Feeling gross internally and extra sticky on the outside, I mustered up a fake smile and ran up the steps to start all over again. *Dear Lord, get me through this.*

Anybody who knows me knows that friends—and I mean real friends—are extremely important; they are like family to me. After two campaigns and winning the election, that premise started to leave me. I could feel it. One of the most alarming casualties in Congress is the loss of humility. As a congressperson, one might not become conceited, but man, oh man, you do become pious, righteous, and judgmental. One of the signs? Congress-critters go through a transformation. You come with lofty goals, and then you start to think that your goals are the most important and only thing. Worse, you begin to think that anyone else's goals are less important than yours.

Worse yet, you begin to judge everyone, and, if their values are not in alignment with yours, it becomes nearly impossible to talk to them. Because you spend so much time pushing your values on others inside Congress with both your own party and the opposing side, it becomes standard operating procedure, even in your circles of friends. It starts slowly, but ultimately, it prevents you from really hearing people and understanding their nuances.

Before I ran for Congress, among my friend groups, I had a very conservative group of old friends who differed with me on immigration, equity, LGBTQ+ rights, and abortion. But during my time in Congress, I stopped hearing them or seeing their side, and ultimately, I drifted away from them. While I will not change my values, I do need to hear them and see them. We are here on this planet to be kind and support each other. Both of those sentiments were eluding me, and I could feel it.

Friendships, particularly old friends, are important, even if you grow apart and are wildly different. After Congress, some of my best and oldest friendships actually deepened while others drifted off. Some drifted that I really wish had not. It makes me weepy sometimes. I am not certain there is a way back. I hope there is someday.

Here are some more observations: I swear on my kids' lives, I have never seen more fawning and social/professional climbing—ever. A particular memory of a White House event still cracks me up when I think about it. Immediately after the Infrastructure Investment and Jobs Act (IIJA) passed in November 2021, I was on cloud nine. My bill, the ASAP Act, was folded into the overall IIJA and another bill I was the lead on. The former was led by me in the House and the wonderful Senator Tammy Duckworth in the Senate. So exciting.

As was custom with big bills, the White House scheduled a presidential bill signing ceremony and invited members of Congress who contributed heartily to the bill. To say I was honored was a huge understatement.

As soon as the buses pulled up to take the invitees to the White House Lawn, the literal pushing and shoving to get to the front started. Standing back, I recollect thinking. *Is this how this works? Members of Congress climbing over one another so they can get good seats on the White House Lawn?* My chief of staff saw my expression and said, "Yup, that is what happens. They sort of lose their minds, but you do need to behave—no laughing at them."

Advancing to the White House, it got much worse. It was like a scene from a high school movie, where a pop star visits the football field and the students rush the stage. I'm not kidding. I decided I would hang back with my friend, Ro Khanna (an absolute mensch, great leader on many topics, and brilliant legislator), and chat while moseying in slowly. He was a great mentor, and we had very similar economic opinions about the importance of innovation and support of entrepreneurs. After the signing, I literally saw members of the House vigorously pushing each other out of the way to get a photo with the president and vice president.

Shaking my head, I walked back to the bus, thinking, *OMG, I'm in a weird Opposite Day movie where congresspeople act like bratty children, and younger adults (staffers) are mature, gracious, and poised. Yikes on bikes!* Almost paradoxically, it is also true that most folks come to Congress to be of service and are there to serve, in a very genuine way. There are many true public servants. Most members of Congress are principled. But the thing that blew my hair back was the true duplicity and constant need for attention; it was mind-boggling. Most members are helpful, kind, gracious, and smart. But for some, *yowza*, the treachery is something to behold.

About six months in, the first knives came out. I had developed a postal bill, based on a former congressperson's original bill, and, in early 2021, a sophomore with some stature and gravitas graciously agreed to cosponsor/lead the bill with me. I was glad to have her on the bill as a coleader. She invited me to a large DCCC fundraiser and asked me for a $5,000 donation from my campaign. I obliged, and right after receiving my donation, she thanked me by stealing my bill on postal reform and preventing it from coming to the floor. When I found her on the floor and asked her why, she would not share a reason. I honestly think she thought this was acceptable behavior. I was gobsmacked and walked away.

At about that time, the battle royale between the progressive caucus and the corporate caucuses (called the "New Dems" caucus, the "Blue Dogs," and "Problem Solvers") commenced over the well-known "Build Back Better" package. During that time, I had begun making progress on my committees on various initiatives, and I was thrilled to contribute. The fighting was relentless, however.

Progressives wanted to address housing, economic inequity, climate, childcare, immigration, transportation and infrastructure, income inequity, and health care. The core group of highly corporatized Democrats and the Republicans did not want to do much of anything, at all, in any way, ever. The inertia was like nothing I had ever seen. In the final week of negotiations, the number of betrayals and lies from Democratic members who took corporate PAC money was beyond dizzying. Ultimately, the most corporatized Dems blew up Build Back Better overnight before it could get to the floor. I was aghast and furious. The lying was breathtaking and, in the end, a spectacular swindle by a small group of conservative Dems. In fact, nine very conservative Dems refused to vote for the bill as is, and as a result, the Speaker relented and took out key pieces related to universal childcare, climate, and immigration. It was significant, infuriating, and set my hair on fire.

That was just the beginning of many betrayals. Smoke signals were heavy and ominous. I began to think maybe I was not the right leader at the right time for this type of work.

One of the first times I experienced bullying from someone I thought was an ally was an attack right on the House floor. I was one of only nine members who voted against the Iron Dome, an amazing technology that is a joint venture between the US and Israel, designed to shield Israel from rockets. Sounds like a positive, yes? Well, it is a defensive weapon, and I agree it prevents loss of human life, a good thing to be sure. However, we had already funded the Iron Dome *fully* in another bill, and Israel was asking for yet more money—a lot more.

In a year when we had challenges on every front with COVID, instead of just saying "yes" to the bill like a sheep, I reached out to my district. I talked to supporters, volunteers, unions, houses of faith, clergy, small businesses, and neighbors. I held town halls. Resoundingly, the answer was "We give them enough money; we need it for other things like COVID, and we cannot play favorites with Israel."

Now, I am a stickler when it comes to a job description. At the top of my duties was this: "to represent my district as their voice" in Congress. The district had made it clear they wanted me to vote no. Unfortunately, that enraged most of the Democratic congressional caucus and the party. For me, it was not a vote against Israel. It would not have mattered the country in question; I felt they should not receive more money when we had just given them a great deal. Within seconds of placing my vote, a senior member of the Illinois delegation and two other extremely pro-Israel members from California literally came charging up to me. "Marie, what are you doing? You cannot vote against Israel. You are putting millions of lives at risk."

I replied, "Actually, I am not. First, I did the research and took the time to find out how my district felt. It turns out that, in addition to the Arab and Muslim American community, all the faith groups, the unions, small businesses, activists, general residents, and neighbors all demanded I say 'no' to the extra money Israel wanted. So, I did."

The congressman shot back, "You will pay for this. The entire North Shore will shut down your support."

I smiled and glared, thinking to myself, *Well, that sounds like an ethics violation for you, congressman, but I will refrain from reporting you because you are genuinely upset, and Israel is your number-one concern. I can see that you are emotional about this. I forgive you because your emotions are getting the best of you. Let's talk when things have cooled down.* The bully group turned on their heels in a huff. Little did I know, this was just the beginning, and ultimately, it was very likely one of the major reasons my career ended in Congress. *Maybe this was a fire I was not prepared for or made to address?*

While I navigated the betrayal and duplicity, I came to know and observe Speaker Pelosi, who is a complex and nuanced woman and leader. While I saw her often when she was leading caucus sessions, the first time I was in a hallway alone with her, I stopped to say hello. She looked up and smiled. "Congresswoman, I understand your dad is not doing well. I will keep him in my prayers." I was shocked she knew and responded, "Thank you. Thank you for navigating us through COVID, the insurrection, and this BBB negotiation." She hugged me, twinkled, grinned, and outstretched a hand to receive a cell phone from her aide. I remember looking at her beautiful four-inch heels, thinking, at eighty-plus years old, *Godspeed, baby!*

Frequently in caucus sessions, Madam Speaker would remind us of the importance of fundraising. This same speech repeatedly started to make my stomach turn by month three. In fact, I really started to ache with the notion that I truly did not belong here. Madam Speaker's speech always started the same way: "We show our power and our values to Republicans by our ability to fundraise." She would go on to encourage vigilance in increasing our fundraising and remind everyone how critical it is to raise money daily. She was a paradox. On the one hand, she was tender and caring. She really did care about the country and children. On the other hand, she was a ruthless strategist and outfoxed the caucus to gain consensus on many occasions. Her leadership during the insurrection was unrivaled, and without her, we likely would have had a very different outcome. I did not agree with her on health care, the Middle East, and some matters of equity, but I will say this: She was and is an enigma to be sure.

Another great figure and party leader was our progressive caucus leader Pramila Jayapal. She is strategic, kind, caring, insightful, tactful, and brilliant. I have always felt that she could be a great Speaker of the House. She led the conversations with the White House on Build Back Better and was a masterful negotiator. Unfortunately, her candor, progressive values, and principles may have prevented her from running for Speaker. She was a steadfast, loyal friend in the darkest of days in the 2022 election. To this day, when she stands up and takes a beating for various stances, I drop her a text or tweet to support. It is lonely being principled and standing up for your values, especially when your own party chastises or punishes you for doing so.

Regarding great members of Congress who I learned a great deal from, two stand out. First, Jamie Raskin, a brilliant constitutional scholar, is masterful at breaking down the Constitution into digestible parts. He is always fair and shares both sides. Jamie is quite possibly the best voice in Congress on legal matters, ethics questions, and law interpretation. He was a leader during the impeachment, and I simply thank him for helping the nation understand the imperative nature of making sure a president is subject to all laws, just as every citizen is. Second, while I have led many teams over the years and have overseen creating a culture on dozens of teams in a wide variety of organizations, I will say Hakeem Jeffries is the best coach/player or servant/leader I've seen in a long time. His political instincts are impeccable, but his timing is prescient. I found his relatability combined with his legal skills, charm, and musical taste to be the combination for great success and a driver of cohesion in the caucus. As caucus chair, he led us to be the most progressive *and* productive Congress in over fifty years. The 117th Congress passed more bills than any other in five decades and successfully governed through an insurrection and pandemic, largely due to his skills. While I disagree with Pelosi and Jeffries on several topics, including dark corporate PAC money, the corrupting and divisive influence of AIPAC, and health-care equity, both leaders were effective and led well.

LESSON: Stick to your values, even when it is unpopular. You will sleep better at night, live a happier life, and not be "owned" by anyone. I believe we get the angriest when an issue we are passionate about is being dismissed or underestimated. Remember, anger is the bodyguard for sadness. When you are overcome with anger, you are merely protecting yourself.

HOW:
- If you are in an all-consuming job like politics, stay close to your dearest friends and folks who hate politics; it will prevent you from becoming transactional.
- Also, get a dog. It will be your only real friend in DC—not kidding.

TAKEAWAYS:
- Don't be transactional or trade ideas, values, or principles for corporate support. Many members take corporate money and are handcuffed for their tenure to those entities. It is the reason we do not have universal health care, a fairer economy, and true climate change.
- The same goes for corporate life. Live your values, be respectful to others, and if your surroundings are not a good fit, move on.
- The hardest thing is to "get over it and move on," yet you must.

CHAPTER THIRTEEN

Your Time to Go Becomes Obvious

GASLIGHTING AND MANIPULATION fascinate me. In politics, both are truly exquisite in their subtlety and brutality. While Machiavellian and vile to the victims, they are also omnipresent and remarkably effective in politics. At the heart of it, the ability to keep telling the same lie with conviction is a tried-and-true best practice in politics. When masters craft it, the victim's own grandmother will believe a ridiculous lie hook, line, and sinker during campaign season.

One ugly, gray morning in February 2022, I had all but decided I was ready to give up and step down from my reelection campaign. I clutched the wheel of my car, pulled over, and it all hit me at once. I started swearing like a sailor, "Fuck these manipulative assholes—I've had it with these people. They do not get to pick the winners and losers! Goddamn it!" I hit the steering wheel with my phone. I realized how narcissistic I sounded and was reviled by my selfishness and self-pity. *Ugh, and double yuck.* Believe me, I know how I sounded.

It struck me head-on: I was missing the joy I felt on my first campaign. My sense of purpose. Working hard and seeing results. Crafting policy that would work in the real world. Being silly with the campaign team. Learning in depth about critical policies. Earning the respect and support of leaders in the progressive movement. It felt like we were all working together. This new primary campaign was about divisiveness and hate. And what was worse, it was within my party. My last campaign was all about being change agents, working directly with the district, having fun, and teamwork every step of the way. Hard-fought policy victories, yucking it up while knocking on doors. Learning volumes of information nightly. Solving real issues.

All of it was a joy.

This reelection campaign was the exact opposite. It was about constantly keeping an eye out for betrayal, sharp knives, and worse. I hated it. When would the next shoe drop? While we had declared a few months prior that I would run for reelection in Congress, I was wavering and thinking about stepping down. Throughout that day, I had a pit the size of a grapefruit in my stomach.

That morning, as I was putting lipstick on and conjuring up the courage to face a challenging day in committee, I received a call from a blocked caller telling me I was a "groomer" and a "socialist cunt." What a delight first thing in the morning! Just a burst of sunshine. Most insults I received were funny. They usually struck me as similar to Jimmy Kimmel's "Mean Tweets." You know the schtick, where some celebrity reads a horrible tweet like "You look like you smell like toe hair," or "Is she a shar-pei or a walrus—you decide."

The week before, I learned that two well-respected Democratic policy organizations, who had been my greatest cheerleaders when I won my election in 2020, decided that "things are getting messy, and folks have told us to stay out of your race"—which I interpreted as "because of your positions on the Middle East, your constant assaults on corporate PAC money, and your semi-socialist health-care views." I thought, *Jesus H. Christ! Medicare for All is not socialist; it combines the government's and corporations' collective strengths as an apparatus.* The socialism thing was the lazy go-to for conserve-o-Dems. Sheesh. It was beyond irritating. Particularly when nearly 70 percent of Americans wanted it! Sometimes, I could literally flicky-finger people in between the eyes to wake them up from the constant conservative-washing.

Over the last few months, one of the hardest and most hateful comments to hear from parts of my own party, media, my opponents' campaign, and their supporters were accusations that I was antisemitic. It was all done in private spaces and well hidden but permeated in a direct and hateful way. My husband is Jewish, but both he and I have progressive values around Palestine and Israel. We had criticisms of the Israeli government, never the citizens of Israel or Jewish folks in general, never. That nuanced view is not well-tolerated by some establishment figures in the Democratic Party when it comes to who they support. I thought about how many times I fought against antisemitism with and without my husband over the last three decades. The betrayals made me tear up every time. I always felt horrible for my husband, as he had to listen to this nonsense all the time. He was a prince about all of it.

Conversely and happily, there were plenty of members of Congress who believed in me and were caring about my dilemma. I will never forget their wisdom or kindness. It was usually the most accomplished, secure, and genuine members who extended support. They were honest about the situation and acknowledged the unfairness and the reality of the situation. I received dozens of calls from people telling me they were proud to know me and that I should continue to fight the good fight. I will always hold those members in deep gratitude. They were gracious and kind throughout the entire primary.

Rewinding the tape four months, it all started when we were in redistricting hell during the final days of October 2021. The state redistricting process was at the end of its work. Redistricting takes place every ten years because of the census. States reapportion each of the congressional and state legislature districts based on the distribution of population. This would be a painful task in any state in any year, but in 2021, it turned the politicking into robust, bare-knuckled treachery, as there was a need to reduce from eighteen congressional districts to seventeen due to population loss. Later, with the state's corrected census, we would find this may not have been necessary, but truthfully, it did not really matter. In the year prior, we met with every expert and state leader trying to decipher the process throughout 2020 and 2021. Everyone in lockstep indicated there would be time for input, the decisions would be public, etc. But nobody ever "knew who was running or actively working on" redistricting. It was a mystery. Naively, I thought everyone would be fair—until the last night of remapping. *It will all be fine,* I kept telling myself. But everything changed that night.

All elected officials, including myself, feel protective about their districts and will fight tooth and nail to keep the communities we were given when we won our seats. This feeling often propels elected officials into ruthless behavior. I just did not understand *how* ruthless. Holy cats, I had no idea what was coming that final night of remapping.

My protective instincts over my district were so strong that I often described them as maternal. Whenever I met with constituents, I felt as though their problems were my problems. When you work through a pandemic side by side with an awe-inspiring set of communities, nonprofits, neighborhood groups, and volunteers, you get emotional and protective about the 750,000 people you are responsible for in that district. I prioritized my time on the ground in our communities, meeting with groups, organizations, community leaders, and constituents. Solving problems together throughout 2021.

I remember early in my term, during the peak of COVID, I received a call from several neighborhood food pantries asking for help. They needed staples like milk, bread, and baby formula. I dropped everything I was doing and called nonprofits, state food banks, and grocery contacts I had. We found the food they needed. My staff helped with pickups and deliveries.

From there, I brought supplies to another pantry at 9 p.m. in frigid weather. The line for food was around the block. I backed my car up and started to unload. A woman from the line recognized me and started to yell, "Government is supposed to help—you are not helping us!" She was crying, with her baby in her arms, overwhelmed. I said, "I know" and wrapped her in a hug. I decided to stay in line and talk to the families until everyone got their food. People were angry about COVID and asked, "Where the hell is that vaccine?" I kept saying, "It's coming, I swear." I heard about many things that night: pay gaps, no money for health insurance, "I lost my job," and the worst, "I just lost my two-year-old to COVID."

I also worried and lost sleep about everyday matters too—flooding, postal delays, food insecurity, the wealth gap, and institutional racism that directly caused inequities in housing, transportation, education, the economy, and more, right here in my district. But mostly I always felt that the buck stopped here, with me. It was my job.

As a result of this almost parental, self-imposed burden, I literally spent all my time doing in-district work. I solved problems with great folks in the communities, but I also became a prolific legislator, setting records in developing and passing bills. But what I did not do was the sexy stuff. I only went on TV when asked. I declined all foreign travel, no matter how fascinating it sounded. I felt there was a huge dearth of problems right here in Illinois. I also neglected to schmooze with leadership—that was likely part of my fatality as a legislator.

Guess what? While that was clearly wrong from a longevity-in-politics standpoint, I think my team and I helped a bunch of folks. I have no regrets at all; in fact, I'm glad. I would do it all again, in exactly the same way. My incredibly talented DC and district staff partnered with the community daily to solve problems. I'm sure they feel the same way.

Back to redistricting. It was the fourth week of October 2021, and the state legislature had gone through six rounds of maps. It was around 7 p.m. on the night the legislature had to approve maps. Based on the state constitution, they were required to approve the maps by midnight, or they would have to extend it to the new year. They were told they had to get a map settled and voted on before midnight. That night, I was in DC and had already been told that in the final map, my district had been eliminated, and I would be in a new mashup district made up of parts of five other districts against a sophomore congressperson from one of those districts. The good news was that the most favorable part of my district-four key suburbs and city precincts would remain in the new district. Sadly, that would change in the coming hours. Regardless, we would be forced into a primary—colleague against colleague. I headed back to my tiny apartment and settled into this idea. I made a frozen dinner and snuggled into my jammies on my couch when I got a text.

The nightmare had gotten worse. In a last-minute and apparently final map at 10 p.m., a very kind friend (there are many kind and brilliant state reps and senators in Illinois, but she was a standout in every way) from the state legislature contacted me, sharing that a final deal "was struck" that had been in the works for weeks. Let's just say state legislators were bullied and pressured by outside forces and some elected officials. It was reported in *Politico* the following day that a member of Congress and his supporters bullied them—and it worked. It was Illinois-style politics at its ugliest. The upshot? My home had been drawn out of my own current district along with four other suburbs where I had a very strong base. I would be losing the most favorable part of my district, and the mapmakers (perhaps forced by others) knew damn well what they were doing. In fact, my home had been drawn out by a mere two blocks. Not very subtle, but they achieved their goal. It appeared the goal was to make it impossible for me to win. Got it! This is the district where I was born and lived most of my life. I was now being drawn into a neighboring district (IL04) where the Democratic member of Congress was well-established, a genuine friend of mine, and I would be an unknown. Further, this was a Latino district with a Latino man serving them. It was and continues to be important for that district to stay a Latino district. Districts must reflect their populations. My choices would be 1) run against my friend in the Latino district or 2) run in the district two blocks away from me that I had just been strategically drawn out of—against a well-established, wealthy member of Congress. I knew I could likely never win if I ran in the newly constructed district, against the conservative, but also would never challenge my friend in the Latino district.

It was clear, at least to me, from the mapmakers and unknown decision-makers that their thinking was this: Newman is the newest to the delegation, she screwed over the former conservative incumbent by beating him in his primary, and she is too liberal. This final map certainly felt like retribution, plain and simple.

This meant that I would be forced to run in a different and newly constructed conservative district (a mashup of five other districts) just two blocks west of my house, against the other neighboring district congressman. I had some awareness of him prior to serving in Congress, and I had kept my distance strategically. I had been warned about him years before. He was extremely wealthy, well-connected, and an amazing fundraiser. He would do anything to win. I was neutral about him as a person; we really did not know each other. However, once he became my opponent, what little I knew about him definitely informed my decision to run against him.

Imagine my unbridled joy: running against a wealthy, conservative Democrat who was more established than me. Fun!

I proceeded to call everyone I knew in the state legislature and ask them *not* to approve that final map. Most were sympathetic but would share some version of "I'm sorry, but . . ." It was unfair, but nothing is fair in politics. Supporters and voters were calling, texting, messaging, and practically skywriting for me to challenge it and run against the neighboring congressman in the newly formed district. I don't think I have ever felt more betrayed in my life. Redistricting in general was fair; it is a constitutional process, and I had no issue with that. This last-minute, cold, calculated, and manipulative political map maneuver that took away a huge base of 20,000 likely votes did not feel fair. Nope, Mama's not having it. My team and I talked through the night about various options.

The redistricting process is constitutionally mandated and expected every ten years. However, in my state, there is no written mapmaking process, at all. None. There is a state law that supports federal redistricting and lightly indicates input from constituents will be received, but there is no defined, accountable, written process, step-by-step. There are no appointed leaders. No process map. No accountability. No who, what, where, and how—at all. Therefore, it is changed and adapted in isolated backrooms every ten years, quietly, with just a few voices. From the outside, it looks like they truly just make it up as they go. As a result, in a postmortem analysis, it is impossible to say the process was fair or unfair because there is no process in writing from which to compare it. Unfortunately for me and my team, the mapmaking and "who to protect and who to screw" decisions were influenced by the legacy of the formerly powerful Mike Madigan, the speaker of the Illinois House for thirty-five years. Madigan hated me after I beat his pal in 2020, Dan Lipinski. Folks, never underestimate the power of potential revenge tactics when it comes to an old Irish politician. His capacity to hold a grudge is something to behold! I can say this with confidence because I am Irish, from the same area, and I watched it for decades.

To be fair, many other politicians and elected officials may be quite happy with the process as it played out in 2021, so I will leave it to future voters and electeds to decide whether this process is the best we can do or if we can do better. In the end, Illinois' process may be good, bad, or neutral, but it actually helped me understand that I was likely not a good fit for politics. I should also share that while I have some questions about the process, I do understand how messy things get and forgive all involved in the mapmaking. I would not want their jobs because they become the sponge for those elected officials who have vendettas and an ax to grind. To be clear, the federal census process is very fair, the concept of reapportionment is fair, and I do genuinely believe it starts with good intentions. The problems come in when all the emotions of various electeds get mixed in a pot during mapmaking. Those who are most established and the best fundraisers are heard first, second, and last. There is no way to not be affected by these angry voices. I forgive, forget, and move on, but I also learn from the experience. Godspeed to all.

Some good news out of this redistricting process? Illinois did carve out a much needed second, additional Latino district and now has a wonderful congresswoman, Delia Ramirez. Silver lining and hooray! For that reason and many, I am glad it all worked out the way it did. All's well that ends well.

After learning about the final map in the middle of the night, we all woke up somewhat bleary-eyed and decided, as a team, I would announce I was running in the newly formed conservative district against my extremely wealthy colleague with an amazing fundraising machine. Further, upon review of the voter numbers and geography of this newly built district, it became very clear: the electorate would vastly favor my opponent. In effect, the new district was custom-built for him. Just f-ing great.

Side note about leadership. When you are a leader implementing an unpopular process with tough decisions, and you have truly bad news coming for some your extended team, the best approach is not to just let each affected team member know about the issue but to also get their feedback *before* the solution is created, include them in the solution-making process, and obtain their buy-in. Next steps include bringing all parties together *before* tough decisions are made (*not after*) to discuss with the folks who are executing plans and those affected. Critical to effective leadership, allow the folks affected by the bad news to offer alternative solutions. This obviously did not happen in the case of redistricting. It is what it is. We moved on. *C'est la vie.*

Having led many efforts, I learned early on when you are a leader, address the issue directly and own it; don't avoid it. Get in front and talk about it early. Strap on your damn big-girl or big-boy pants and don't be a baby about having to deliver bad news. It's called being a good leader. Also, avoiding taking the reins is malpractice and childish. In the redistricting example, nobody would take the reins, and it was allowed to proceed chaotically. It became inappropriately contentious. A lack of leadership always creates chaos. Leaders who run from taking the mantle to protect themselves from the negative outcome are not leaders. This is the problem in politics: There is very little leadership but a great deal of avoidance, hiding, passing the buck, whining, secrets, and deceit.

To be clear, the leadership no-nos were the hallmarks of the redistricting process. There was finger pointing and nonsense but no accountability or ownership. Oh well, good lessons for history and a cautionary tale for those campaigning during redistricting in 2030-31! Ultimately, it provided an escape hatch out of a business I was not suited for, so things truly do happen for a reason. Good management, facts, honesty, and leadership matter. I am an optimist and hope things will be more transparent in the next redistricting process. I wish everyone well.

For the next four months, we had meet-and-greets, toured businesses, and visited community groups. While most major unions and progressive national groups stood with me, money would be a problem. We worked hard, and I fundraised daily. As predicted, we simply could not keep up. I was validated in the 100 or so meet-and-greets that we had strong support. I remember one new supporter in a large town hall meeting saying, "That was utter bullshit that they drew you out of your own district by just two blocks, and worse, making two colleagues fight it out is reminiscent of the *Hunger Games*. Marie, you *are* this district. You get it. You are the real one." My opponent had strong DCCC supporters, and I did not. I was the outsider, and everybody reminded me of that, daily. The boulder my team was pushing up the hill kept getting heavier.

While my fantastic campaign team and I had built a resilient coalition of organizations to run with me and support my reelection, the groups and folks working against our campaign were growing, and

I knew it. As early as January, a dear friend told me their organization, a longtime ally, was "going to have to endorse against you, and gosh, we are just so darn sorry."

In fact, the pile-on was just beginning. I was told this would happen. Organizations with whom I had a long track record—progressive folks, donors, elected officials, and counselors—told me, "I'm staying out—it's too messy; your opponent will be well funded by conservative and adversarial organizations and, well . . . he and those groups are, well . . . ruthless." Other donors and supporters said, "They are going to torture you unmercifully. He is going to run you over with money." I remember having coffee with an older member of Congress, and she stared at me with piercing seriousness and said, "You know what your problem is, Marie? You are not willing to go for the jugular, and worse, you are far too transparent. You cannot tell everyone the whole story, every time. It does not work that way here." I was miffed, but I knew she was right. My head felt dizzy, and my heart was heavy every day. I just plowed through the best I could. Was I being a blind idiot? I gotta tell ya, yeah, I was. There was no way to win this thing.

Back to that February day (three months into the reelection campaign) in my car, I made it through the day without quitting. It was now early evening. I sat in my little Honda crying and trying to decide whether to shut down the campaign or keep going and deal with running against a huge pile of money and power. Central to my worries were my opponent's potential and super PAC rumored to be getting ready for battle against me, the weaponization of my progressive philosophy and votes, huge corporate money, a manufactured scandal outside groups cooked up, and then the folks who only care about how much money you raise. *This could not go well.*

Alternately, the other major consideration was that I loved my teams—on both the campaign and government side. We had become quite close. I loved my district. I felt like the district's mom, and I simply could not leave them. I could not fathom being responsible for the fifty team members across my congressional offices and campaign losing their jobs because of me. I could not fathom anyone else partnering with my district. The community leaders depended on me. The weight of it made me want to curl into a ball and disappear. I wasn't sleeping, I gained weight, and I could not find anything but highly manufactured joy each day.

In addition, the constant tug of not addressing my family's mental health issues was killing me, and not softly.

An insidious thing happens to elected officials: your world simultaneously becomes huge and small. You are working twenty-four seven with acquaintances, staff, meeting new people daily, by the dozens, yet frequently feeling alone. You neglect and ignore friendships and family. Selfishness becomes "necessary." Or at least you tell yourself so. It makes me cry when I think about how often I missed major events or tragedies because "duty called."

One of those times was early in my term. We put my dad in hospice care, and my sister called to say, "You should come and see him." I knew what she meant. I flew to Arizona and spent four days with my dad, who was highly sedated and in constant pain. When I arrived, all I could think about was how thin he was, and his formerly huge flop of thick hair was all but gone.

For the few days I was there, my mom told me sweet stories about their dating life, and we looked at old black-and-white photos. They were such a cutie-pie couple. My dad had intense blue-gray eyes. I had always wished mine were that color. I tried not to cry in those last days with him, but frequently I had to "take a call outside" to keep it together and cry in the hall alone. I remember the last time I saw him alive. I said, "I love you, Dad, so much, and you are the best, the best." Unfortunately, I did not say that nearly enough to him in the years before.

I regret that deeply.

His death hit me in waves for months, catching me by surprise, usually when I was in a great mood. I would see, smell, or hear something that brought me back to my dad. Walking to the Capitol in late March, I smelled the cherry blossoms along New Jersey Avenue. They looked gorgeous, and I smiled. Then, unexpectedly, I launched into an ugly cry. I knew what it was.

A year earlier from that fateful day in my car, my dad succumbed to his battle with conjunctive heart disease. He was a fighter, three and a half years in palliative care and two months in hospice. When he died, I had no time to mourn. I was three months into my first term when I saw him last and did not know he would only live one week more after that visit. I did not say enough. I did not *feel* enough. It was rushed. Watching your parents waste away to nothing is gut-wrenching. When they are freed from that agony, it is not any better.

His funeral was intimate, and it hit me like a cement wall. There was a church service for family, and then the military flag ceremony really got to me. I sobbed. The soldiers folded the flag with great precision, walking toe to heel in rhythm, slowly, and with intent. My dad was really dead. I just could not get my head around it. It was my job to place his bronze urn in a special memorial slot. I slowly secured it in its eternal resting spot.

Suddenly, I spit out an uncontrollable gasp and said, "Oh God, Dad, I can't believe you are gone. I love you. I love you so much. I can't—" My legs buckled, and I clutched the cold cement shelf. My husband grabbed me and held me up. We went back to my sister's house, sat on her patio in the warm April air in Arizona, and reminisced. We told stories. My dad was very reserved, which made him all the sweeter to me. My mom missed him terribly already; we could hear it in her voice. She told us dozens of stories. We laughed more than we had in a long time. It was the first time we had all been together in years. It felt warm and like home.

The next day I raced back to DC for an important vote, pushing his death out of my head for back-to-back meetings, hundreds of pages to read, debates, speeches, presentations, etc. I literally could not process his death; I was way behind, so I got to work and didn't look back.

It was a shortcut. I do this. I move up, out, and over bad feelings. I've become adept. I do not feel the necessary feels; I just move on. That is my standard operating procedure.

That night in February, I watched the snow land on my car's hood outside of a campaign event. I was parked at a church to meet voters. I was late (as always). To make matters worse, I had to tell my daughter that I could not help her with an important paper she was working on. My failure to spend time with my family was becoming a heavy blanket I couldn't ignore. The snow was coming down hard, with a strong Chicago headwind, but once I moved my gaze to the asphalt, I noticed it was melting as it hit the ground. I'm a big fan of signs, even small ones. Seeing the snow melt was enough to wipe away my tears, reapply makeup, and get my behind inside that church. Even the heaviest snow drifts succumb to warmth. I smiled at the thought.

Nick, my reelection campaign manager who had been with me for five years, met me at the door. He whispered, "Are you okay?"

I said, "No, but when the hell has that stopped us before?" We snickered. I knew this room was filled with lovers and haters of my opponent. Here. We. Go.

LESSONS: Leaders are clear, compassionate, and objective. They should not play favorites or seek retribution. When a leader hides, it means they are wrong and know it, or they are cowards. Don't hide. Share your process, analysis, and reasoning. When something is inevitable and will be a life-defining bitter pill, brace for impact. Appreciate those around you who willingly and righteously stay by your side during a tumultuous ride. They all matter, and they need to be thanked daily.

HOW:

- In every prolonged, tough, and exasperating situation, plow through. Take each day one at a time, keep your eye on the

prize, and keep going. Even if you lose the fight, know you will have learned something amazing along the way, and it perhaps was meant to be, so you are free to find the direction or place you are better suited for in the future.
- Think of a tough fight as a marathon, pace yourself, know there is an end with an answer, and you will be able to rest and have peace in the end.

TAKEAWAYS:
- First and foremost, be an adult, and when you have bad news, share that news clearly and in person with all the affected parties *before* decisions are made. Include them, don't disrespect them, and keep them out of the process.
- Seeing the goodness in the moment is a hard lesson. Feel the feels. Even though the calm does come eventually, it can be preceded by grief and failure.
- Remember this: The calm defines the road ahead and allows you to build a new dream. Hope has now arrived. Get ready for it.

CHAPTER FOURTEEN

Seven Brutal Months

I DECIDED TO ROLL the dice and keep going after early notions of considering stepping back from the reelection. February, March, and April of 2022 were grueling. The incessant rumor mill, ongoing fabricated BS, and scandalization of an internal ethics review were really starting to take their toll on me, my staff, and my family. It was brutal. While congressional campaigns are known for their rough tactics, mine was one for the record books. It was well-known that a conservative coalition in Congress wanted to get rid of progressive Democrats, and I was top of that list in the 2022 cycle.

This conservative coalition worked hard to make certain I was not reelected. To be clear, this is standard operating political campaign procedure when either your own party wants you out in a primary or the opposite party in the general election wants you out. Political coalitions are built to do everything in their power to prevent you from having a successful campaign. In my case, redistricting did not go my way and placed me in a very conservative district I was not suited for. I angered conservatives by speaking out against corporate PAC money, I constantly pushed for universal health care, and I had progressive positions about the Middle East. On top of all of that, there was an ethics complaint registered with the Office of Congressional Ethics by an outside, conservative group. All of these things worked against me. The good news for me was that in the months after the primary election in 2022, the internal ethics complaint review was closed and finalized, with no violation cited, as we knew it would be. The bad news? It was a very convenient thing to point to by my opponents during the primary (the review was conducted during the primary and closed post-primary). Additionally—and conveniently—I was a progressive running for reelection in a conservative district custom-built for my opponent. For all those reasons, my campaign became untenable quickly.

This has to be said: For those considering running for Congress or any office, understand you have a target on your back twenty-four seven. *Psst*, you think it won't happen to you, but it will. I say it in the kindest way, but please, please, ladies, if you run, do not be naive like me. Still run; I'm not discouraging you at all! I am a full advocate, but know what you are getting yourself into and what to keep an eye out for. In Congress, anyone—literally any person, group, or coalition—can send a complaint armed with inaccurate, out-of-context, or erroneous information to the OCE (office of congressional ethics, a nonpartisan group inside the US House that decides whether a complaint should be reviewed by the ethics committee or not). For nearly any reason, a person or group can direct a complaint to the OCE, who must review it in thirty days. The OCE receives roughly 3,000-6,000 of these per year, and many are referred to the House Ethics Committee for many reasons, including limited staff and bandwidth. Mine was. Fascinating to note, when I was in the US House of Representatives, there was no HR department, and there had never been such an entity. No really, not kidding. Typically, in a for profit or nonprofit company, employee issues are addressed by the Human Resources department. In Congress, there is simply the OCE and the Ethics Committee assigned to review these matters. There are pieces of standard HR department operations spread across other staff and committees, but there is no single HR department at the US

House of Representatives. Wild, right?

Critical to note, while I was incredibly angry with the Ethics Committee because of the stress, anxiety, and work induced by them, I know they were just being thorough and following the rules of the US House and Ethics Committee. As I look back, while they were exhaustive in their examination (often to a point of repetition and extreme frustration), working diligently on it for well over a year, they truly were just simply doing their job. We, of course, gave them more than they needed and were extremely cooperative. The committee was doing the job that should have been done by the OCE, in my opinion. While I have lots of specific questions regarding the practices of the OCE, their role, potentially breaking rules, and not following their own procedures, conversely and importantly, the actual House Ethics Committee was highly professional, competent, and exhaustively thorough. They indeed followed the rules to a "T." This, of course, was painful. The committee and staff were always very respectful and polite, but not friendly or kind. In other words, they did their job incredibly well and professionally, even though, honestly, they frustrated me to no end. We knew the matter would be closed with no citation, as it ultimately was in late 2022, but the process was so horrifying and humiliating, I actually sought therapy, something I had never done before.

I will never forget the day after I was referred to the committee, when a conservative publication's reporter all but accosted me and followed me for blocks, yelling, "Don't worry, Newman, we will take you down." I walked home thinking, *Does this guy think he is living in the middle of an old-timey private investigator movie? This place is an absolute freak show sometimes.*

One of my more startling realizations was that certain opinions are literally forbidden and are not welcome inside Congress or by certain outside groups. When one does not toe the line on "third rail issues," one may be punished by one's colleagues—and by outside groups. One of those issues was the Palestine-Israeli issue. At this point in the

2022 race, I received the first of many threatening texts from folks who opposed me on my progressive Middle East views. One was from a former supporter and a longtime AIPAC supporter. After I voted for a resolution that acknowledged the existence of the Nakba, the night in 1948 when 700,000 Palestinians were expelled from their homes by Israeli militia, a text popped up on my phone: *"Marie, I was extraordinarily disappointed to see that you cosponsored the Nakba resolution and aligned yourself with Rashida Tlaib. To date, the pro-Israel community has remained neutral in your primary. This (sic) changes that."*

And, holy cats, affiliates/members of AIPAC, the Democratic Majority for Israel (DMFI), United Democracy Project, and their networks came out of the woodwork in force, right away getting to work against me.

Within that month, that group started crafting a campaign against me. They used persuasion campaigns against me with groups who supported me (either indirectly or directly on the ground), by gaslighting anyone who would listen and supporting my opponent vigorously. This group included affiliates and members of AIPAC, United Democracy Project, the DMFI PAC, and several other affiliated PACs supported by conservative Democrats and Republicans. Other groups involved in the negative campaign were very conservative Democratic donors and PACs with funneled money (through channels and related PACs) from the notorious and convicted felon, FTX CEO, Sam Bankman Fried's PAC (his brother, Gabe, had been previously employed by my opponent and was his DC staffer for a year prior). They all had sided with my opponent. I knew they would. Truly, it was sickening, but honestly and objectively, it was quite impressive to watch. Also, all of this is legal. The vitriol from these groups and my opponent's campaign ripped me and my family apart from limb to limb, emotionally, for months, contributing to mental health issues we are still dealing with. Their vigilance, rancor, and hatred of me was remarkable. The ungodly amount of money spent characterizing me as something I was not, was simply chilling.

Politicization of any issue, misogyny, racism, scandalizing standard internal processes in Congress, sharing inaccurate information, making one's opponent out to be unethical or monstrous—it is all fair in love, war, and politics. These types of shenanigans are perfectly legal and happen daily in political campaigns. Political speech of almost any kind is largely legally protected in campaigns. Honestly, most other opponents would likely have done exactly the same thing. It is what it is. I was determined to run this race even though I knew the odds were almost comically stacked against me.

Oh, but just wait, folks, there's more.

It all just about broke me. Previous supporters were moving away or staying neutral because they knew I would be out-fundraised four to one. Money always wins, always.

They were right though.

A bright spot I hung onto was that women's groups (Emily's List, NOW, women labor leaders) were still fighting with me. I will never forget these progressive organizations' moral codes and kindness. All Godsends. Love them. They helped me plow through every day.

There were many kind members of Congress who had been generous with their time, wisdom, and financial resources on the campaign side. Congresswoman Ilhan Omar, Congresswoman Rashida Tlaib, and I frequently commiserated in the cloakroom off the House floor about various smear tactics that the conservative wing of our party and Republicans employed to keep us from speaking up on universal health care for all, economic equity, getting corporate PAC money out of politics, and the Palestine-Israeli issue. They had been through ethics reviews similar to mine by the Ethics Committee when outside groups registered complaints against them. Hmm—is there a pattern here? Maybe a step-by-step process to make sure there are only moderates and conservatives and absolutely no members focused on working families or humanitarian rights in Congress? Not sure, but it all looked darn familiar, and clearly I was not the first to be on the receiving end of this behavior and set of tactics. I admired how these women handled the ridicule, smears, bullying, and treachery. They not only worked incredibly hard and were effective legislators; they also took time to help others like me. I am so grateful for their support and kindness. Many others were kind, respectful, and helpful as well. They will never know how much their smiles, encouraging words, and direct advice buoyed me during those dark days.

About ten weeks to Election Day, when we fielded our poll, we were tied. After months of work by legions of wonderful volunteers knocking on doors, making calls, sending postcards, and visiting small businesses, community groups, and neighborhoods, it was good news to be tied. On that same day, we learned that my opponent's super PAC, propelled by affiliates of DMFI, other pro-Israel and pro-corporate money PACs, which typically supported very conservative corporate Democrats, were setting up shop to work *against* me and *for* my opponent in the final eight weeks of the campaign. The irony was DMFI supports incumbents, and both my opponent and I were incumbents. DMFI decided to support my opponent because he was conservative, supported Israel fully, and had corporate backing. Pro-Israel lobbies like DMFI and related super PACs had been extremely powerful and were very successful during the 2022 cycle at targeting progressive Democrats and eviscerating them with unsavory campaign techniques. They took me down, but also several other congresspeople and other great candidates in that same year. They were merciless. For those who don't know, a super PAC is a political group who can raise unlimited funds and run a full TV/print/online/mail/field/media/one-on-one/phone campaign either for their candidate or against their candidate's opponent but are not allowed to directly coordinate with the candidate's campaign. Again, it is all legal. We can thank Citizens United and a conservative Supreme Court ruling for that bucket of fun, which empowers billionaires to literally fund and purchase elections, all legally.

I will let you guess what happened. Yup, the super PAC kicked my ass all day long, for weeks and weeks. It was humiliating and really affected my family, staff, and me. Five weeks out from the primary, we were down seven points. Their ads called me everything you could possibly imagine. And worse, while most of it was untrue, the opposing team also seemed to be gleeful whenever my family was hurting badly. One time on an airplane, a member of my opponent's team actually invaded my privacy several times in a wide variety of truly creepy ways, including listening to phone conversations, taking screenshots of my laptop, and calling their colleagues to laugh about me and my family. I will never forget the lack of humanity. I knew this would not end well. My opponent's super PACs and affiliates spent nearly $1.5 million against me, and my opponent's campaign was outspending me four to one. I will never forget the film-noir-style TV ads they concocted, dripping in red and black lighting, with a voiceover reminiscent of Will Arnett's baritone pipes, in guttural tones, spouting how unethical I was. It is funny now, but then it was utterly humiliating, and worse, there was nothing I could do because we lacked the funds to take it head-on with a counter campaign.

Our opponent's campaign had also turned many folks against me with a months-long whisper campaign (this is done on most campaigns), a constant barrage of salacious emails, event speeches, publicity campaigns, interviews, and my opponent simply maligning me at every chance he had on TV, radio, events, and on social media. As I said, gaslighting is truly amazing when done well. Some of the whispers were hilarious. A group of my opponent's top supporters and surrogates had shared, with a straight face, in a room filled with donors and supporters, that I snorted cocaine, was having an affair, mistreated a donor, and took or gave a bribe (it alternated, with very entertaining stories). Seriously, look at me. I am the poster child for dork moms from the suburbs. Sweet baby Jesus, I was incredulous over this crazy-town rumor campaign. Again, all legal. It was very well executed and precise. And it worked.

My opponent's campaign utilized their top donors/supporters in health care, business, nonprofits, and the party to assail me. I was aghast by the sheer venom and spiteful behavior. I just don't have that level of hate in me and am incredulous when I see it up close. A few of my opponent's top supporters had real axes to grind because I dared challenge a wealthy White man in his fifties.

Even worse, because of the smear campaign about a "scandal" both my opponent and his super PAC were shouting about, militia groups, full-on wackos, and creepy folks were threatening me, daily. My family and staff were taking fire from all sides. Constantly. I was frequently stopped by militia-lite folks and screamed at with awful threats. There was not a day that I did not think someone could shoot me, run me over with a car, or attack at any time. The right-wingers lobbed threats in public spaces, like "We are taking you down. You will pay for this, and we will find you, Newman. You should be fucking scared."

There were days when I just wanted to quit (read: every day). The constant hate and violent threats were merciless. I ended up not sharing a good deal of the threats with my staff or family; they had enough bad news on their plates. But I was terrified. On one particularly bad day, a young woman ran up to me in a conservative and new part of the district and said, "You antisemitic, Nazi bitch. You kill babies. I hope you and your family die." I thought for sure she would pull out a gun.

A week later, folks came from a meeting where they heard wealthy conservative donors in the new district call me a "loudmouth socialist bitch who was a sad sap for poor people, and oh yeah, I hear she is unethical too." The whisper campaign, the negative TV ads, direct mail, the news articles, the online pounding of official-looking and ridiculous ads about "an investigation," and the ongoing salacious emails from my opponent's campaign were quite effective.

Sadly, most of the hate was generated from dark parts of my own party. Those folks did not like my votes on economic equity and health care for all, being vocal against corporate PAC money, stance on Palestine/Israel, and some working families-related votes and positions. A small group of conservative Dems, who were supporting my opponent, were angry and wanted me out. They let me know it. I was surprised by the animosity. It was surreal.

Alternately, and happily, my volunteer army, supporters, and voters stayed with me from my old district. Thank God they believed in facts, truth, transparency, ethics, and authenticity and understood the role that money and power were playing. If anyone ever questions the right thing to do, honesty is always the best. It will carry you through the worst of times.

While I was angry, this behavior was legal and part of the game. Campaigns, candidates, PACs, and super PACs can tell partial truths, embellish, reshape information, use defamatory language, share slanderous speech, and be cruel, but there is very little, if any, legal recourse when you are a candidate or an elected official. Also, to be honest, most campaigns would do exactly as my opponent did. By extension, the super PAC supporting him and his supporters did the same. This is the norm and not unique. The misogyny, gaslighting, and treachery are omnipresent in campaigns everywhere.

I am proud to confirm that, in all three of my campaigns, I fought hard and even viciously on policy, opinions, positions, and voting history, to be sure, but I never, ever, maligned my opponent personally, his family, or his character on a campaign publicly, even though we had well-documented ammunition. We were presented several times with clear evidence of my various opponents' long lists of legal, criminal, and ethical questions/issues/receipts, and we were asked frequently to use it against them in all campaigns. I'm very glad I did not. I sleep well at night and have no regrets. Folks, always play the long game.

Critical to note here is this: AIPAC, DMFI, United Democracy Project, and the Democratic Party leadership have a large problem. Simply, AIPAC, United Democracy Project (UDP), and DMFI are creating a substantial division in the Democratic Party. AIPAC and DMFI are viewed as bullies. Everyone in Congress fears their wrath and ability to infuse tens of millions of dollars into primarying them. Just in the last two cycles, these two PACs and their affiliates have taken out twelve incumbent and challenger Democrats in primaries, simply because they had progressive stances. I would respect AIPAC and DMFI a great deal more if they stood up for Jewish Americans regularly, stood against antisemitism, and worked to send relief money to Jews around the world as their mission. This is not the case, to be clear. They spend money on hurting elected officials politically and zero dollars on helping people in nonpolitical situations. Every time these PACs enter a race, they character assassinate the candidate who does not bow down to them, and honestly, I do not remember so much as a mention of Israel in any of their campaign ads. So really what is their mission? My observation is that they believe that by taking out every progressive and semi-progressive Democrat in Congress, they will be able to control the party and, ultimately, Congress. Is AIPAC, UDP, and DMFI's goal to make Congress fully conservative or centrist because those folks can be fully manipulated by controlling their campaign money? I feel it is. Democratic Party leadership needs to start grilling these groups on their interference and bullying—and do it now.

The new challenge for AIPAC and DMFI moving forward is that they can no longer claim anyone who dares to call them out for their bad behavior as antisemitic. People have caught onto this tactic and are not buying it. This is their go-to for anyone who says anything negative about them for any reason. It was difficult for them to call me that because I have a Jewish husband and a long track record to refute that antisemitic label. It would also be hard to call Kamala Harris antisemitic for the same reason. Her husband is Jewish. These groups with fealty to Israel's war-mongering behavior are particularly egregious when there is plenty of real antisemitism in the world they should be addressing. That said, the Democratic Party leadership will need to reckon with this divisive and bullying behavior from these groups, or there may be some disastrous outcomes. A third party could be developed, a party civil war could prevent the party from governing in coalition, an unveiling of bad behavior around the undying support of Israel (fealty to a foreign nation is generally prohibited, apparently except for Israel) and how this horrifying behavior was condoned . . . all of these could be revealed, and the public would very likely revolt. Finally, because AIPAC and DMFI frequently attack women and people of color in campaigns, they could be looking at questions of misogyny or racism. Just as ominously, many young Democratic and middle-aged voters say AIPAC and DMFI are starting to have the same type of reputation as the NRA. Not helpful in a party where we are trying to be inclusive. My hope is that AIPAC and DMFI will have new leaders soon who will look at things fairly, advocate for both Israel and Palestinian people everywhere, and stop their support of the far-right groups in the Israeli government who approve of the slaughter of innocent Palestinians. Right now, their positions are hurting Israel and Jews across the world, and as a result, Israel is becoming isolated and disdained internationally. Their model is only preventing important progressive voices from being heard; people are being hurt and voices squelched. I hope they choose fairness, equality, and equity, not divisiveness, moving forward.

Back to the primary. Two weeks before, the saddest day of all came. It literally made everything else fall away. It appeared out of nowhere, like a hammer. My opponent's daughter died suddenly in the middle of the night. She was only seventeen. I could not imagine the unspeakable horror for that family. I was a mess when I heard. I went home and shut down. Nothing was as awful as losing a child, nothing. The election no longer mattered at all.

The campaign was over, and I knew it. Immediately, we decided to be positive and shut down all media, negativity, and heavy lifting. We just let the campaign wind down softly and kindly, with no more fight. We decided to have fun, be kind, and take it slow to the end. My heart broke for my opponent and his family. That night at home, my husband and I poured a glass of wine, sat on the patio, and thanked our lucky stars for our many blessings. I watched my sweet beagle run around with his bunny doll. He always knew when I was sad. He came over, licked my leg, and hopped up on my lap as if to say, "I got you, Mommy." Caressing his velvet, soft ears made me feel better, and for the record, for me, it's much better than any antianxiety medication. I save a lot of money on medication!

Nobody deserves to lose a child, never, even someone I was very angry with at the time. We shut everything down on the campaign and let the chips fall where they may. It was over. I knew it, but the Universe or God was trying to tell me something.

My opponent won by a huge landslide, but in my grief, I also felt relief and gratitude. I had been an absent wife and a missing parent to my adult children, who needed me more than ever. I have always said that God really must be clear with me when he wants me to stop walking through fire. Subtlety does not work with me. I will keep walking, taking fire, and getting burned until I am presented with four cement walls, several explosive devices, an army of special ops fighters, and a hydrogen bomb. Anything short of that smoke signal would simply not work if I wanted to keep going. *Don't worry, God, I got it this time.* I'm done, for real. Also, I felt immense gratitude because the brutality was over, and I was glad to be done. I was also grateful to have been defeated. It truly ended up being a blessing.

It was over; I would be a one-term congressperson. I was proud of the tremendous work my team and community had collaborated on. We made history repeatedly. We brought more money into that district in one term than any other prior representative and passed more laws as a freshman than any other rep in that specific district in one term in recent history. I was proud but incredibly disappointed and felt like a complete, overwhelming failure. I let everybody down.

My husband took me on a five-day hiking trip after the election. It was the perfect antidote to a great loss, but it also meant I would need to be quiet with my feelings, feel the sadness. I'm not great at this. I like to move on quickly, up and over the bad stuff, not feel it, and then get busy avoiding it. This time, I did not have a choice. I had to feel the failure, betrayals, and guilt and accept the loss for what it was: a sign. Smoke signals made it clear. I needed to stop walking through fire. I needed to get out of politics. Like the wise lawmaker told me months before, I simply was not tough enough, and I was far too transparent.

While I had "started over" many times in my career as a marketing executive, management consultant, antibullying expert, nonprofit founder, small business owner, community activist, and gun reform advocate, I never had a full-on failure in those roles. Here was a full-on *fail*. I knew the universe was telling me I was needed elsewhere. But where?

In the end, I know I would not have shifted gears on my own, without that clear signal, but I am happy to report that I am grateful now. It was necessary to fail for me to move the hell on. My feelings were layered and indiscernible. *Am I mourning? Am I glad? Am I relieved? Am I resentful? Am I filled with remorse and regret?* It was so confusing for weeks and months.

Importantly, the right person won this district. My opponent was much more conservative and in greater alignment with the newly created district. He was willing to do whatever was necessary to win, and I simply was not. I endorsed my opponent, supported him by asking my voters to support him, and then stayed away from the race so he had full room to win the general and do things his way. The election was fair. I had no quibble with that. We wished him well and still do to this day. While there are three critical issues that I disagree with him on, it is up to the voters to make decisions about candidates, not me. Voters choose leaders. I am comfortable and supportive of the voters' wishes. Fair is fair.

I did know a few things for certain. I lost my election, damaged my relationships, and was responsible for my team losing their jobs. I was devastated, but it stopped me from getting further burned and ruining my life. Losing helped me understand I needed to move on.

For the first time in five years, I was calm and not looking over my shoulder. The days' quietness was welcoming. I will be forever grateful for the tranquility and lightness of each day.

Getting over this would prove to be tougher than I thought, but I did. The campaign's vitriol and lies affected my daughter and husband significantly. They suffered from depression and anxiety and had severe mental health relapses. My daughter started showing signs in May.

In the weeks after the election, I was busy helping her regroup and get back on track from her episode with depression, but I also knew something else was looming. The nagging feeling of my husband's telltale signs of depression and anxiety were no longer something I could ignore. I frequently caught him staring off into nothingness, and he was constantly disengaged.

For months, he had not been terribly interested in social events, his mood was neutral, and he was uncharacteristically short-fused. One morning several weeks after the election, I woke up feeling better, like I could take on the world. I bounded downstairs with a pep in my step and found my husband crying. There is something absolutely soul-crushing about seeing your husband cry. This six-foot-plus man, formerly captain of the football team, with an easy smile and soulful green eyes, my favorite boyfriend for three decades, was weeping uncontrollably. I knew what was next. He looked at me and said, "I'm going to need your help, honey." I held back tears and hugged him harder than I had in a long time. I did what I always do—I started solving right away. I put the bat signal out via texts and calls for help. My friend, Mark (a CEO of a nonprofit behavioral health organization), helped us get an appointment with a psychiatrist that same day. I will never forget that kindness. Mark and his husband are among the treasured folks I met along my journey in politics. I will always love them extra.

The good news was that I was finally there for them again. My family needed me, I was present, and I was their problem solver. I felt like I could make up for my mistakes and sins of the last few selfish years. After months of therapy, a recalibration of meds, dog walks, hugs, and the best conversations we'd had in years, both my daughter and husband were thriving. Mostly because they are complete rock stars and dug deep in their souls to get better. Their grit is inspiring. I will not take credit for their hard work; I was just happy I could be there to help.

This loss/failure was a big ol' fat sign: I was needed elsewhere, and I had some work to do to make up for my lack of presence with my family. But what were the other lessons?

Forgiveness is a superpower. Forgiving folks who lied about you, lied to you, betrayed you, or worked collaboratively to "take you down" is not easy. Forgiveness has to be authentic. I was filled with anger for weeks but finally decided that my blessings are so incredibly bountiful that I could not stay angry. I have many friends, a full life outside of politics, and my family's health. And not having to worry about safety and security for my staff, my family, or myself was soothing. It hit me: The torture was over, and it was time to forgive everyone.

With blessings, gifts, and a . . . new challenge on the horizon, it was like the sun came up on my life. Forgiveness came, and it was bountiful. And genuine.

When overcoming loss, grief, or failure, forgiveness is healing for oneself, but it also helps those around you so they can be empowered to do the same. Also, it is absolutely okay to have a layer of complexity in the process of forgiving. When one soulfully and authentically forgives someone, it is still okay to note and be aware of who they really are. They showed you who they were when they lied, broke your trust, or collaborated to hurt you. If they are willing to lie, backstab, and cheat their way to achieve a goal, they are humans, and you still need to forgive them. They are who they are. You can forgive, but it is also okay to not respect them or trust them. However, it is critically important to stop hating them. I create a neutral zone around folks like that. Don't spend time thinking about them. Wish them well and move on. You and others will heal faster. And, after time, sometimes folks can regain trust. Not all, but some. Be open-minded. I am. Equally important, don't let them hurt you again.

Counting one's blessings is transformative. I had an epiphany the day after the election: *Oh my gosh, I never have to call people and ask for money for my campaign again! Woohoo!*

So, what the heck was this immense, tangled, and highly integrated ball of hell meant to demonstrate to me? I took the signs and started searching. The smoke signals from the universe said, "Get in, lady, we are going for a ride. You have a lot to figure out." So, I did.

LESSON: Forgiveness is the first step in healing. There were only a few folks who were truly despicable during this campaign, but it took me several months to forgive them. I did and am stronger for it.

HOW:
- The first step after a big failure or disappointment is to believe it and feel it.
- The second step is to accept it happened for a reason.
- The third step is to know that this was the universe's sign to find a new role and purpose. You are needed somewhere else.
- This is where my workbooks, "A Life Pivot, Made from Scratch," "A Family Mental Health Organizing Plan Made from Scratch," or "Starting a Small Business Made from Scratch" might be helpful for you. All on marienewmanstudio.com.
- After something like this, consult the Life Grades Chart in the pivot workbook. You will need to rebalance!

TAKEAWAYS:
- Don't let me dissuade you from office, but be prepared for what can happen!

- Stepping up to run is noble, and there are many noble folks in government.
- Sometimes life hands you a bag of garbage, sent to teach you something, so take the time, be humble, and learn.
- Do not ever be afraid to lose a job while standing up for your principles; you will feel better in the long run, I promise.
- Your best first step is to forgive. Take the time to do it authentically and truly.
- For your own mental health, you do not have to like or respect the person/groups who hurt you; just learn not to hate them. Neutralize your feelings and move on.
- Once you forgive them, find your way and find your bliss. But you don't need to be friends with folks who hurt you. If you can, wonderful! But not everybody is worthy of your friendship. Sometimes it works. It is A-okay if it does not.
- Move on! But don't skip the feels coming off a big sadness, disappointment, or loss. Feel it. Be present. Let it run its course and start building again. You will be stronger.

PART FOUR

Lessons in Letting Go and Growing

CHAPTER FIFTEEN

Choosing curiosity, not fear.

WHEN I WAS very young, I loved the painting style of Monet because of the ethereal and mercurial look of impressionist art. It was soothing. As I aged, I started to really like the clarity and reality of Edward Hopper because it was more literal and relatable. I knew the subjects in his work, and they resonated with me, but I also knew the landscapes, coffee shops, bars, neon signs, and busy streets. As I get older, familiarity feels better, whereas new and different used to.

I knew one thing: the familiarity of my friends and family gave me great comfort, but I did really need to clear my head!

On our postelection hiking trip to Asheville, North Carolina, Jim and I experienced gorgeous mountains, a laid-back city center, beautiful weather, and lots of quiet time. It was the perfect medicine, but as we know, medicine usually tastes bad. Toward the end of the election, my brilliant husband knew this and planned a hiking trip with pristine landscapes, where I could hike for hours and "feel the feels." I needed to not skip over them, but I did not like it, trust me.

As I hiked in those beautiful mountains, I could see the last five years of political work behind me and started to feel actual relief with stillness and sadness.

When people say some gifts come wrapped with several layers of thorns and stinky garbage, it is true. Knowing the gift is in there is what gets you through the layers. My gift was realizing my family needed me, and I had gotten through a bunch of the gut-punching layers.

When I had my small business, I used to gaze out my home office window in search of answers. When we came back to Chicago after our trip, I looked out my window for a long time. It felt good. I liked staring out at my messy collection of untamed grasses, perennials, 100-year-old trees, and really pretty weeds that I kept out of beauty and laziness.

Being at home with no drama was soothing. We had dinner with close friends. I could meet girlfriends for cocktails. While I was perennially nervous about "what's next," I was also living a little. Something I had not done in five years.

"Care less, love more," shared my dear friend, Paul, at dinner one night. He was right. Not caring what people think and loving more was working. I truly felt forgiveness toward all. However, and I stress this, it's important to be open to trusting again.

At fifty-eight, I learned my most important lesson thanks to my husband and friends' constant harping: You can't trust everyone. Who knew? I now know and will never forget. Oh, and authenticity is everything. Be who you are even if it means leaving a job you love.

Finally, tenacious hope. God saved this sophisticated emotion just for humans. Cultivate and feel hope regularly. Forgiveness comes when we understand others and ourselves. Hope comes when we see the light and possibilities.

Real life is truly the best mentor. Thank you, life. Thank you, family. Thank you, real friends. Thank you, acquaintances who made me think. Thank you, thank you, thank you.

Now, finding a job. Ugh! Meetings, interviewing, and networking. I had not interviewed in seventeen years. My days were filled with folks offering ideas, jobs, positions, etc. I was overwhelmed. Going into the last days of 2022, I felt like the world was whirring while I was being plunged into a hole in the space-time continuum. It was uncomfortable yet necessary.

Unpredictability and gray areas are not my faves. However, whenever I have embraced that feeling, I often benefit. This time was no exception.

Executive recruiters were prolific with opportunities, but *I just could not decide* what the heck I wanted or should do.

Ultimately, it came down to a public affairs/marketing firm president role or a CEO spot at a large nonprofit. I chose the large developmental disabilities nonprofit.

Why? Because, I had not done something like that before. New and different felt right. While I felt genuinely connected to the mission because two of my cousins had developmental disabilities, I don't think I ever felt as passionate about it as I should have. Honestly, one of the things I feared in taking the role was that I would grow restless after a certain amount of time.

I learned a great deal in the year I was there. Employees at nonprofits are like great parents. They stay through thick, thin, and everything in between, even if it is hard on them. My admiration for these folks is immense. My education there was robust. Often, the middle managers were the most knowledgeable about the programs, services, and residents. They were kind enough to impart great wisdom for months.

One of my first memories after taking the CEO spot was during a visit to several of our residences on campus; the house manager took me aside and shared that the turnover of the direct service professionals (one-on-one caregivers) was their greatest problem. They kept losing folks because of low pay and the difficulty of the work. The residents and participants in the day programs who receive this care feel soothed by consistency and repetition. When a caregiver leaves, it is traumatic. I spent a long time talking, listening, and learning the same lesson over and over. The direct service caregivers at disability residences and day programs are a combination of God's helpers, care experts, and saints who love unconditionally. These folks have to work with residents and participants who are often unwilling to move, acting like toddlers, and lacking control of their bodily functions. They love and keep loving those they are assigned to, no matter what. It is astounding. Unconditional love is a good life and professional lesson, no matter who you are. I still reflect on these team members and smile. I will always feel proud of the Human Resources team for their passion to work with me to bring these God's helpers a pay increase and more days off. I felt it was the very least we could do.

During my time there, the executive team and I reorganized the entire organization, balanced their books, increased fundraising, and built a real culture, all within the first few months. It was fulfilling work and a good challenge.

The first thing I noticed the very first week I was there was that nobody would talk to each other. It was stifling. Like many organizations, during COVID, culture died because everyone was siloed and never in person. Nobody's fault. Nobody was developing relationships and working as a team. At the end of the first week, it was clear I needed to require people to come back to the office at least three days a week. They did, begrudgingly. Early days, I started visiting the office buildings around campus, and I would pop in and say hi to folks throughout the day. This was a new concept. Team members found it surprising. Over time, folks started enjoying it. They started talking to each other. When I heard more giggling and chatting in the hallways, I knew we were getting somewhere with culture and team vibes. Loved it.

The tougher lessons? Not everyone likes to be managed the same way. I set up accountability metrics for all departments. One of the teams was not excited about this. Some acquiesced, some actually loved it, but others did not. Those folks revolted. I was firm and pushed hard. In the end, I likely should have just kept the peace, let it go, and let those folks who did not like accountability have some more latitude, but because I am all about fairness, I pushed everyone the same way. In the end, I think I was not the right fit for the organization. This happens, and knowing when to move on is important. I no longer felt passionate about the cause, but I cared and wanted them to succeed (and still do). So I decided to leave, but when and how?

My most important life lesson? Folks with disabilities (visible or invisible) also have invisible abilities we can all learn from. Keep your eyes and ears open to it, and if you hire them, your organization and life will be changed for the good. Trust me, hire folks with disabilities. It will bring you amazing emotional and financial dividends in your organization.

My most important professional lesson? I likely was not a good fit for most nonprofits because I do push hard, sometimes very hard. Second big lesson? Trust was an issue with a few ancillary folks, and I knew things would not go well after that. My dad had a saying: "Once someone has broken your trust in a major way, they will do it again. They have revealed who they are to you. Listen to that and learn who they really are because they will continue to operate in the same way." Trust is very hard to establish after it is lost, so I took it as a sign to move on. Still, I felt very good about the new programs, increasing the number of folks in our care and augmenting revenue, so I felt I had accomplished a great deal and could move on. Probably the change at that organization that most excited me was the huge leap the employment services team made in job placement for our residents. We doubled the size of the program, and we were placing twice as many folks with disabilities in jobs than ever before. Bravo to that team! The nonprofit was thriving before I came, and after I left, I genuinely felt the team and I had significantly improved its sustainability. I still root for this wonderful organization and am excited to see them grow. I have nothing but compliments for the whole organization, and I'm so proud to have been a part of it for that year.

It was a lovely experience and a wonderful organization, but I grew restless. About six months into my tenure there, this book was still unfinished, and it was bugging me. It was like a constant whisper in my ear. I thought about deleting it or—alternatively—working on weekends, making it different or shorter. But like a constant love, it stayed with me, and I could not get it out of my head. I also realized I was going to need to make a change soon, as I had done many times before in my life. The team at the nonprofit organization was smart, wonderful, and hardworking. We accomplished a great deal, and there was still much to do. However, when you are a "changeaholic" like me, if you have worked with a team and solved a bunch of problems well, you will feel your job is done, and it is hard to keep addressing the same problems week after week. I needed new challenges. I knew it was time for me to go about ten months in.

About eleven months in, I realized I did not want to fundraise every week. After a year, I resigned and took on a few contract project clients to help give me time to understand what I should do. As in romance, the disabilities organization had been my "bridge," not my forever love. It was a fantastic "palate-cleansing job." For the record, my predecessor was a great leader, left a wonderful foundation, and there were many talented folks there. It was a great team, and I truly admired them. That experience allowed me to learn new things, meet great people, feel good about humanity, and get away from politics. It was a blessing. Now, what to do?

So here I am, with a self-imposed pivot. Writing the next chapter of my life.

These are the challenges of a card-carrying "changeaholic." You grow restless in the best of situations. Only a small percentage of the world is a changeaholic. Changeaholics are always curious and open to the next thing. Conversely, most people in the world fear change to some degree. I could learn to be more content and stay in one place; it would be helpful to everyone in my orbit—believe me. I tease my husband frequently, "You know I am fairly good at family/friend relationships, but not so much with employers. I tend to move on when bored. You and my close friends are the only relationships I have stuck with more than a few years." He always laughs and says, "Well, lucky us."

To that end, my next pivot is unfolding in interesting ways. I know a couple of things. If I can help anyone who is struggling with a pivot or building something from scratch, I am here for them. Fear of pivoting is the obstacle. The need to pivot is simply the universe and your subconscious telling you it is time to grow and expand your consciousness. Or some cause or somebody needs you.

Guess what? The universe is pretty much always right. Your mission, when you feel this tug, is to reflect, research, understand, and refine where the tug is coming from, and then go to it.

LESSON: Nothing (except love) is really forever. Sometimes, after a huge disappointment, great sadness, or setback, a "palate-cleansing" job, event, or trip helps you understand what you want and need. It is a stopover with a lesson. You will learn a great deal, and just remember, nothing is forever except those you love: family, friends, and of course, doggies!

HOW:
- When transitioning into a new phase in life, it is A-okay to try something new, even if it is not the ultimate fit or solution. In fact, it is recommended.
- Stop and take stock. Know how you got to where you are, know what you would do differently moving forward, and think about what you want in life.
- Take a peek at learning something new or take on a big personal challenge.
- My " Life Pivot" or "Building a Movement" planning guides might help you when reassessing life, career, or passion projects.

TAKEAWAYS:
- It is okay to take a job you know may not last forever!
- Be okay with the stepping-stone nature of it.
- Operate from curiosity, not fear.
- Be open to doing something that is not quite your mojo; it might actually be what you want or lead you somewhere positive.

EPILOGUE

This is a Happy But Different-Than-We-Thought Ending

SO, WHERE DID this crazy, circuitous road lead me to? Well, for starters, I jumped right into completing this book (and had a great deal of fun with it) and wrote the corresponding workbook series to help folks start their own "made-from-scratch" life solutions, whether it is a social impact movement, a job, personal challenge, a political campaign, mental health plans for families, supporting transgender kids, or a new small business. It is now complete and will be available in tandem with this book. Additionally, I'm having a heck of a lot of fun consulting on public policy and public affairs for clients. I joined a few boards. I'm also enjoying helping young entrepreneurs and social movement leaders get their organizations off the ground. I am feeling incredibly grateful for all my friends who extended great love over the years as I figured out my purpose and what I should do when I grow up. Gratitude and blocking out cranky people is truly its very own high. Yay! Even more so, my appreciation for family and friends who helped with our family's health-care challenges is more than I can ever articulate. Our whole family is managing our emotional and mental health as a team, doing well, and we are blessed to have each other.

In the end, and I just came to this recognition recently, I am not intended to do just one thing! So how does that work? Well, I decided to take my time, start writing more, daydreaming more, and laughing more. And yes, you guessed it. I spent a lot more time with dogs. After I took stock of what I really wanted, everything got easier. I decided to not only finish this book and the workbook series but start a fiction novel (watch for more news on this on my social media in 2025). Accordingly, I started my Substack.com column, @marienewmanstudio, which comes out each week on Wednesdays, and I will be collaborating on a storytelling podcast in 2025 as I continue to help start-up businesses and social impact groups.

In my free time, I am still volunteering on campaigns I feel passionately about. For those movements working on health care for all, getting money out of politics, gun reform, and women's rights, I am still a fan and still working out there for them as well.

I share this notion of pursuing a "portfolio of work" because, for many of us, we want to have a few "gigs" or part-time jobs and blend in some passion work on the side. Had I not failed in politics, I would not have been able to pursue these opportunities or see them unfold before me. I truly have no regrets and would do everything exactly the same; even the mistakes facilitated this very happy landing for me. I'm a lucky duck.

We all follow a different roadmap; just make sure you have one—loose or tight.

In closing, I offer this: be open to the world, ideas, and 180-degree turns. Most importantly, be empowered to build your "made-from-scratch" solution. You got this!

For all these reasons and more, I decided to formalize a system I have used for years to solve problems and create change: "the life made from scratch" methodology. This approach helps folks 1) assess where they are, 2) get their dreams in writing, 3) develop goals, 4) research their ideas and find key resources to help their roadmap, 5) problem solve, and 6) create a tangible plan toward your goals.

For extra credit, each booklet lists more extensive resources, should the reader wish to dive deeper into the topic. If you think any of my workbook planning guides can help, they are all available at marienewmanstudio.com or Amazon:

A Life Pivot Made from Scratch: A workbook that helps folks think through where they are, what they need to do, and how to create that change or pivot.

A Family Mental Health Organizing Plan Made from Scratch: A resource that will help you organize your loved one's treatments, activities, supports, and work toward gaining better mental health. **Disclaimer:** this workbook helps families support their loved one—it is not a health care or mental health advice booklet—merely a guide to help a family get their information organized in support of their loved one's mental health.

Building a Movement Made from Scratch: Assists folks interested in creating a movement, social campaign, or social impact organization, with a roadmap to develop something made from scratch in service of their goals.

Starting a Small Business Made from Scratch: A planning guide designed to help folks get their dream to have a small business off the ground. It includes the research development, business plan model, etc., needed to start your own business.

Supporting Your Transgender Child, Made from Scratch Planning Guide: For those parents or guardians who have learned their child is transgender or nonbinary and are wondering what to do. This will help you get started. My personal experience in this space will empower you to understand what to expect and how to handle it.

Building a Political Campaign Made from Scratch: Campaign planning and structural tools for folks considering a run for office or candidates for public service.

Now, as each of you begin your life solution journeys, here are some things to know and think about:

When a female friend says, "I can do anything a man can do," tell her she does not need the last four words . . . at all.

Be just as grateful for the wounds, burns, and scars as you are for the good times in your life. It makes you more robust, multidimensional, empathetic, fuller, smarter, richer, and wiser. Good times make you love life. Hard times make you understand it from a perspective you had not planned. Sometimes fulfillment comes in hard-to-take packages.

You have to be intentional with friendship. Particularly after forty, I believe that most women pursue friendships (likely unconsciously) because they believe they can learn from them, be uplifted by them, feel good about themselves, or truly admire them. Friends fill holes. Be purposeful in choosing friends and make sure you are filling the right holes with the right people. If friends are not equal parts supporting you and letting you know when you need course correction, expand your circle; you need both. Time is short. Invest in people who are worth it.

Envision your dream before you start moving toward it. Then you will have an image as a North Star to follow.

Accept and know when you are not the right leader for a job, even if you have done an outstanding job in that role. When everything points to your defeat in that role over time, listen, digest, understand, and accept that you are no longer right for that role. Find your next fire. Nothing lasts forever. It is a-okay to fight for that role, but know when to move on as well.

When a challenge comes your way, one that nobody else wants to deal with, ask yourself this: If I don't do something about this, who will? If you are pretty sure nobody will, guess what, baby? The fire found you; it's yours. Jump in!

Sometimes the extent of a problem is not really known, but as humans, we usually try to avoid owning problems that don't "seem like they are ours to own." But here's the thing: When everybody is walking around the weird, gross, sticky, smelly ball in the middle of the room, pretending the stench does not exist, it's a problem.

Sometimes, you have to pick up the gross, sticky ball and assess it. Don't be afraid to assess a problem, even if you decide it is not yours to take on; you should always try. It will be another great lesson on the journey.

Kids are supposed to have unexpected, hard-to-understand problems. It is their job. Their sole purpose is to learn how to be a human, and your sole purpose as a parent is to take care of them, guide them, and help them to do the same for their kids.

When kids blindside you, just know they are doing their job really well. Take the challenge with gusto! Kids always keep lots of fires on hand, so wear protective gear and bring a hose everywhere you go.

DIY, baby. Make it from scratch! You will find from time to time that a job, an industry, a product, a life solution, a philosophy, a treatment plan, or a service that you perceive is needed and important does not actually exist. Guess what? The fire found you again. You have now been called to do-it-yourself! Be the DIY queen you are, and make it from thin air! Your very own real life is one of your best mentors, so get up and get that thing built.

Mentors are critically important. I can tell you that when I have pursued mentors and taken the time to learn from them and develop a genuine relationship, I have been at my best. When I have neglected to do so, I have failed.

Enjoy the journey, and I'm rooting for YOU!

- Marie

www.ingramcontent.com/pod-product-compliance
Lightning Source LLC
LaVergne TN
LVHW041810060526
838201LV00046B/1193